Comp@Central

An Anthology of CCSU Student Writing from Writing 100, 105, and 110

2023–2024

XanEdu

ISBN 13: 978-1-71147-158-7

Cover: © Can Stock Photo Inc./kudryashka

XanEdu

17177 Laurel Park Drive
Suite 233
Livonia, MI 48152
800-562-2147
www.xanedu.com

Contents

Dear Composition Students,

This *Comp@Central* essay collection was designed especially for you. It contains outstanding essays from your fellow students at Central, which they wrote in the very same composition classes you're in now. The essays in this collection were nominated by professors and selected by a committee of English Department faculty members, and they reflect strong (though not perfect) writing from students in composition classes during the 2019–2020, 2020–2021 and 2021–2022 academic years.

We hope you'll view this anthology as more than just a reader as you develop your own writing skills. Your professor may assign certain essays and use them during class time, but you can also refer to *Comp@Central* for models and inspiration. Every piece in the collection makes an original argument. And the collection includes samples that illuminate complex parts of college writing, such as drafting original thesis statements, synthesizing sources, and organizing longer arguments. So, take notes in the margins. Highlight, underline, and circle parts of the essays that you might want to emulate or ask questions about. This is a resource for you.

The anthology is organized by genre: analyses, arguments, and reports. The analysis section begins with an essay by Cedric Westcott, who argues that Bojack Horseman—despite being an animated horse—represents human, raw, wrenching, struggles with addiction and mental illness. Kate Masciadrelli's essay about Ed Dante's defense of ghostwriting provides a nuanced example of rhetorical analysis. Masciadrelli demonstrates Dante's persuasiveness, while ultimately citing problems with Dante's ethos and tone. The last piece in this section analyzes an essay by Kenneth Goldsmith about whether people waste time on the internet. The student author, Maslin Laberge, examines the effectiveness of Goldsmith's tone and appeals to logos, but views the appeals to ethos as underdeveloped.

The argument section leads with Nicole Gonzalez's essay about transgender representation in the media; this essay argues that while representation has increased in recent years, it is not yet on par with other demographics, even those within the LGBTQIA+ community. The next essay, "More than Role-Playing: A Virtual World," by Victor Setaro, responds to the lingering belief that video games lead people to violence in the real world. Setaro argues that research showing this causal link is lacking, and the essay encourages readers to appreciate the benefits video games have for many. The next two essays by Aaron Saindon and Marc Perras can be read as a pair. They take opposing positions on whether the United States was right to withdraw from Afghanistan in 2021. The last argument essay is by Ashton Peterson, who advocates for both employees and employers to take job satisfaction seriously. This essay shows the complex factors that lead workers to dislike their jobs and it demonstrates the wide-ranging impact the problem has on individuals and businesses

Finally, the collection ends with one research report by Eric Klem. This paper is an example of writing in a formal genre, and it compiles existing research on the effect anxiety disorders have on high school students' academic success. The report utilizes standard sections for sharing research across disciplines, including an abstract, methods section, and discussion section.

We've carefully curated this collection to be helpful as you develop particular writing skills. A new volume gets published each year, so you have an opportunity to be published here in the future!

Sincerely,

The CCSU English Department Composition Committee, 2021–2022

Dr. James Austin
Dr. Elizabeth Brewer
Dr. Amanda Greenwell
Dr. Eric Leonidas
Dr. Melissa Mentzer
Professor Clementina Verge

Analysis

Bojack Horseman—Most Human Character on TV

Cedric Westcott, Writing 110

Scrolling through Netflix late at night, it would at first glance be difficult to distinguish animated adult comedy *Bojack Horseman* from the seemingly endless supply of formulaic, bland, and often tone-deaf animated comedies that plague the streaming service. *Bojack Horseman* is undeniably a comedy, and its jokes and humor alone are strong enough to catapult the show into elite comedy status—but as funny as the show is, it prioritizes detailed characters and storytelling above all else, all while still finding more than enough opportunities to make the audience laugh. Rather than showing us a constant string of barely related episodes that exist almost independently of one another (i.e. *The Simpsons*), the show's episodes are all installments in a continuous and multifaceted storyline. The show's main lead and title character (voiced by Will Arnett) is a middle-aged, half-man half-horse who formerly starred as the father in the lighthearted and beloved fictional 90's sitcom *Horsin' Around*.

The Bojack that we are introduced to from the show's very first episode is a stark contrast from the lovable character he portrayed on *Horsin' Around*. Bojack suffers from depression and is overall an extremely insecure and self-destructive character who regularly abuses drugs and alcohol. Throughout the story, we are exposed time and time again to many of Bojack's worst decisions; these are rarely just referenced briefly in the show's dialogue, but shown on screen to us, the audience. In Emily

Nussbaum's (2018) *New Yorker* article "The Bleakness and Joy of "BoJack Horseman", she references the show's "built-in risk," writing "as effective as BoJack is as a character, he runs in circles. That's what addiction is, after all." As much as Bojack wants to right the wrongs that he is responsible for, he continuously tries to escape his pain time and time again by going on alcohol or drug-fueled binges that inevitably result in even more damage to himself and others.

The COVID-19 virus has been a terrifying example of a worldwide health crisis that we can easily see the tangible symptoms of; but lurking under the surface of COVID lies a dangerous predator that is not so easily seen. In "Stupid Piece of Sh*t"—a *Bojack Horseman* episode from Season 4—we see this aspect of invisibility in mental illness portrayed with a very unique and effective approach. The episode focuses on Bojack's internal monologue (still voiced by Arnett), beginning with him lying in bed while calling himself a "Stupid piece of shit" along with other insults. Much of the episode continues in this same fashion, with Bojack mentally berating himself repeatedly and imagining unrealistically dark and negative ways that others view him. The belief and thoughts that others hate him or that they think he is a bad person only furthers his internal monologue's abuse of himself, and he tries to get away by going to bars as well as sitting in his car doing nothing for hours on end. He interacts with other characters via normal dialogue throughout the episode, but these scenes are interspersed with his own thoughts, showing the viewer how hard it can be to tell what is going on in someone's head.

While we can tell from someone's external symptoms such as coughing or high temperature that they may be physically ill, it is much harder to know when someone may be suffering internally. Mental health is an increasingly severe issue in our country, with Mental

Health America (2021) citing an increase of 1.5 million adults who experienced a mental illness between 2017 and 2018. These are numbers from well before the pandemic, which has itself contributed to an even further increase in rates of depression, anxiety, and suicidal ideation according to a 2020 report by the CDC. Stigma and negative assumptions surrounding mental illness are certainly not things of the past, but there are major strides being made to help reduce them. A survey conducted by HealthPartners (2020) in Minnesota and Wisconsin in 2017 and 2019 shows that the Make It OK campaign—which seeks to educate people about mental illness and reduce the stigma surrounding it—has drastically increased the percentage of people in the observed regions that would be willing to talk about their mental illness, tell a friend if they had a mental illness, or seek help for their mental illness.

The term "mental illness" has been used numerous times throughout this essay already, but I would like to briefly clarify what it can mean. Much like the wide variation in physical illnesses, people battling mental illness are not dealing with one condition; they can be experiencing symptoms from one or more of a long list of different disorders. *Bojack Horseman*'s representation of characters with mental illness does not stop at just Bojack with his alcoholism, frequent addictions, and depression; fellow lead character Diane Nguyen, (voiced by Alison Brie) is a writer who suffers from anxiety and depression throughout the show, and Bojack's mother Beatrice (Wendie Malick) has a particularly hard to watch struggle with dementia. There is a vast range of severity and variation in disorders under the blanket term "mental illness," and these specific conditions are not mutually exclusive. Recent years have seen numerous celebrities including Demi Lovato, Dwayne "The Rock" Johnson, Billie Eilish and many more come forward with stories of their own experiences battling mental illness. Seeing and hearing celebrities that we idolize talk about their personal struggles with mental health can be an extremely powerful tool to both help those suffering to realize that they are not alone, and to show that mental illness is not about strength and can happen to anyone.

A large part of what makes *Bojack Horseman* so different from other shows or even comedies about substance abuse and mental illness can be seen immediately, from Bojack's very own appearance. Issues such as depression, anxiety, addiction, and other forms of mental illness are problems that are uniquely human. Bojack himself however—along with many other characters in the show—is very clearly not a human at all. Rather than creating a show about a middle-aged man struggling with human problems such as mental illness and addiction, this world shows us a horse with those same human problems; and the absurdity and uniqueness of this replacement of man with horseman makes the same story far more interesting. As entertaining as it may be to watch an irreverent sitcom or an emotionally moving drama, *Bojack Horseman* introduces a new layer entirely by somehow managing to be both at the same time. It is this careful tightrope walk between being a realistic, important drama about mental illness and addiction and being an absurd comedy that makes the show so different from anything else quite like it.

Characters in *Bojack Horseman* are not always what they appear, and *Time's Arrow*, one of the show's most heart-wrenching episodes late in Season 4 is a perfect example of this. The episode, being almost entirely from the perspective of Bojack's dementia-ridden mother Beatrice Horseman, is in a very different format from the majority of the show's episodes. Taking place late in season 4, Bojack's mother has until this point been portrayed as a cold, uncaring mother who played a huge part in shaping Bojack to be the damaged and emotionally scarred (horse) person that he is today. This episode displays that coldness in the older version of Beatrice, but also shows us another version of Beatrice; it shows us a younger character who once had aspirations and dreams of her own, a character whose good intentions and hope (like Bojack) eventually crumbled away after years spent in the presence of either a cruel, uncaring father or an emotionally distant husband. And the present-day version of Beatrice shows a broken character so ravaged with dementia that she can no longer even distinguish past or present. Bojack Horseman is not a show where you can easily place blanket labels such as "good" or "bad" on its characters, and this episode is one of the absolute best in the series at displaying that.

With depression, mental illness, and society's overall awareness around them having risen in recent years, it makes perfect sense that a show like *Bojack Horseman* became as popular as it is. Whether the show draws you in with its humor or its realistic and unrefined depiction of grief and depression, one cannot help but leave each episode wanting to know what will happen next. From his opioid-fueled choking of fellow costar Gina Cazador (Stephanie Beatriz) on set of a show to convincing former *Horsin' Around* costar Sarah Lynn to break her sobriety to go on a bender that ultimately leads to her death, it is no longer easy to see Bojack as the protagonist that we have come to expect most main characters on TV to be. However the audience ultimately views Bojack and the other characters by the show's end, it is rare to see a show—lest of all a comedy—provide this level of complexity to a character guilty of such horrendous actions. While Bojack is of course a fictional character, it is not hard to come up with very real examples of people who bear many similarities to the mentally ill substance abusing horseman himself.

Following the divorce of Johnny Depp and Amber Heard in 2016, an increasingly ugly and drawn-out series of court battles has gone on between the two actors stemming from Heard's allegations of abuse against Depp and the resulting article from British newspaper *The Sun*, which referred to Depp as a "wife-beater" (Marshall, 2020b). As a longtime fan of Depp's acting, a part of me would like to believe that these allegations are false and that the person whose work I have so long admired has never been violent toward Heard or other women. However, between Heard's allegations as well as the court ruling in 2020 which backed up these said allegations with "overwhelming evidence" of Depp physically assaulting Heard on twelve occasions, I find it harmful and delusional to try to claim that Depp is somehow an innocent victim defending himself as so many of his supporters continue to do. This battle between the two stars is and has been an extremely public affair, and many fans of both actors are quick to fervently defend their favorite of the two celebrities while often completely vilifying the other.

The many Johnny Depp fans who continue to blindly idolize him despite evidence of his past violence towards Heard astounds me, but this examination of the two celebrities' tumultuous and drug-addled relationship is not intended to condemn or support one or the other. Depp has claimed that often the physical altercations between himself and Heard were instigated by her rather than the other way around, with him sometimes leaving the room and trying to distance himself from Heard during arguments in an attempt to prevent the situation from escalating (Marshall, 2020a). Several of Depp's claims have themselves been supported by witness testimony, further muddying the waters on just how accountable each of the actors is for the violent incidents in their relationship.

Ultimately, it is pretty much meaningless to ask the question of whether Johnny Depp—or Bojack Horseman—is a good or bad person. Like Depp, Bojack is a famous actor who abuses alcohol, drugs, and sometimes women. Unlike in Depp's real-life situation however, in *Bojack Horseman* we as the audience see the inside information that leads to these self-destructive or otherwise harmful actions; we even see that Bojack does truly appear to be remorseful for causing Sarah Lynn's death, choking Gina, and attempting to have sex with Penny (the 17-year-old daughter of his former love interest Charlotte). His self-loathing and regret involving these actions does not excuse them or make him a more sympathetic character, but offers a rare look into the mind of an abuser that we do not get to see in real life.

Works Cited

Butler, Bethonie "Celebrities are talking more about their own mental health. It's helping — even if it's complicated." *Washington Post*, 2020.

Czeisler et. al *Mental Health, Substance Use, and Suicidal Ideation During the COVID-19 Pandemic* 2020.

HealthPartners (2020)"Stigma of mental illnesses decreasing, survey shows".

Hess, A. (2018). BoJack Was Made For This Moment. The *New York Times.*, 168(58108), 1–2.

Marshall, A. (2020, July 25). A Court Battle They Could Both Lose. *New York Times*, 169(58765), C3.

Marshall, A. (2020, November 3). Johnny Depp, Called a "Wife Beater," Loses Libel Suit. *New York Times*, 170(58866), C3.

Mental Health America (2021)"The State Of Mental Health In America".

Nussbaum, Emily "The Bleakness and Joy of 'BoJack Horseman'" *The New Yorker*, August 8 & 15, issue 2016.

Rhetorical Analysis of Kenneth Goldsmith

Maslin Laberge, Writing 110

It's likely that when *Homo habilis* sharpened the first stick into a spear, one of his fellow cavemen complained about the good old days when clubs were all they needed. In the countless millennia since, human technology progressed considerably, always with similar debates about its use. In his article, "Go Ahead: Waste Time on the Internet", Kenneth Goldsmith advocates for the titular message. He argues that 'The Internet' is not a singular beast, but countless different things for different people (and even for the same person). Considering that this entity can serve almost any purpose, it cannot be generalized that being on the internet is wasting time. He brings up numerous oft-spoken criticisms towards being online and points out how they don't stand up to scrutiny and how the nay-sayers don't acknowledge the usefulness. Goldsmith's use of tone and logos provide a compelling argument that time on the internet is not wasted but this could have been strengthened with a stronger use of ethos.

Goldsmith's article was first published in mid 2016 for the *Los Angeles Times*. As implied above, he seeks to alter opinions by providing reasons why the internet is not a waste of time. The general attitude towards the internet in 2016 is fundamentally the same as today. In the developed world, everyone except Luddites and the Amish make use of it and it's effects reach them regardless. More specifically, Goldsmith is referring to casual usage: portable devices, social media, and web browsing, which is the typical consumer's engagement. These are all things any reader would be familiar with, particularly the adults who would be reading the *L.A. Times* who consider their children/friend/colleague to be always online and wasting their time. Due to the assumed familiarity of anyone reading, Goldsmith is able to take a more casual tone throughout the essay, providing relatively simple arguments that the readers will be able to understand and hopefully relate to.

Because anyone who frequently uses the web has heard the same criticisms repeated time after time, Goldsmith is able to mimic this by using a somewhat frustrated and skeptical tone. The opening in particular emphasizes this, "When I click around news sites, am I wasting time because I should be working instead? What if I've spent hours working, and I need a break? Am I wasting time if I watch cat videos, but not if I read a magazine story about the Iran nuclear deal?" (Goldsmith 500). His barrage of responses to the question of the internet being a waste of time provides immediate skepticism towards the "common knowledge" and provides examples of his point that the internet is multifaceted. Additionally, it makes him appear on the defensive, despite having arguments for his point, which feeds into the feeling of frustration. Further along, he brings up another point, "I keep reading—on screens— that in the age of screens we've lost our ability to concentrate, that we've become distracted. But when I look around me and see people riveted to their devices, I notice a great wealth of concentration, focus, and engagement." (Goldsmith 501). By emphasizing "on screens," (Goldsmith 501) he shows that even those who claim this modern technology is bad are using it to spread their arguments. This apparent contradiction helps the reader to also feel skeptical of such claims, as does Goldsmith's immediate followup, calling the point into question. This pattern of giving a common complaint and then Goldsmith arguing against it is used throughout the essay, which in addition to providing reasons for his point, gives a feeling of frustration.

Besides conveying tone, this providing of reason invokes logos, which is critical for anything but the most immaterial arguments. Naturally Goldsmith does make use of it, providing reasons why a given criticism falls short. "And I keep reading—on the Internet—that the Internet has made us antisocial, that we've lost the ability to have a conversation. But when I see people with their devices, what I see is people communicating with one another: texting, chatting, IM'ing" (Goldsmith 501). He provides a common objection to being online and gives rationale as to why the reader should doubt it. However, his use of logos couldn't be considered flawless. As shown by the previous quote, Goldsmith uses anecdotal evidence for his arguments, rather than rigorous logic and scientific studies. This does serve to make the article more approachable for the general public which it was written for. Furthermore, while anecdotes may be outside the realm of pure logic, they're still evidence. Because internet usage is omnipresent for any reader, they could also look at people in public or ask their friends and potentially have Goldsmith's beliefs about it's flexibility affirmed.

Related to the topic of anecdotes vs formal studies is ethos and Goldsmith's use of it. As previously stated, ethos is used fairly weakly. Goldsmith's casual tone and personal anecdotes invokes the feeling of an acquaintance giving their opinion. While this makes his essay readable for anyone with a copy of the *L.A. Times* or his book, it doesn't provide a reason why he would necessarily be correct. His credentials are only mentioned in the author blurb rather than the work itself, which may not have been present in the original publication. Goldsmith does provide a quote from Marshall McLuhan which helps his point, but fails to mention McLuhan's credentials as a modern philosopher. If he had added a reference to a formal study that casual usage of the internet can help with reading or communication skills (just as an example), then readers would have more reason to trust his overall statement that the internet isn't a waste of time.

Goldsmith additionally makes use of pathos, although perhaps not as frequently. If the reader has a preexisting attachment to using the internet, then any argument in it's favor would feed off of that and strengthen Goldsmith's argument. However, such readers wouldn't be the ones who need convincing. Goldsmith dismisses the emotional appeal that internet critics uses, but uses it himself several paragraphs later "After reading one of those hysterical "devices are ruining your child" articles... The daughter responded indignantly that she wasn't just 'clicking around.' She was connecting with a community of girls her own age who shared similar interests," (Goldsmith 503). His use of the word hysterical shows that the opposing article should be ignored, while his reasoning gives his argument value. Goldsmith's use of logic makes his use of "think of the children" stronger than the one he's criticizing, allowing use to turn this cliche emotional appeal for himself.

Overall, Goldsmith's skeptical tone makes his writing more casual, which fits the general audience it was presented to. This also means his arguments aren't as hurt by the lack of hard evidence. Goldsmith's use of tone and logos provide a solid argument that the internet shouldn't be considered a waste of time, but a greater use of ethos would provide more reason to trust him. All of these parts allow him to persuasively present his argument in a way that's entertaining to read.

Works Cited

Goldsmith, Kenneth. "Go Ahead: Waste time on the Internet". *They Say/I Say The Moves That Matter in Academic Writing With Readings*, Edited by Marilyn Moller, W.W. Norton & Company, Inc, 2021, pp. 582-586.

Ed Dante
"The East Coast Ghostwriter" Analysis

Kate Masciadrelli, Writing 110

In "The Shadow Scholar," writer Ed Dante uses his personal experience as a ghostwriter for a custom-essay company to demonstrate the extent of cheating present in the higher educational system and to make the controversial claim that the educational system is failing its students by focusing on grading rather than helping students learn. Consequently, students are forced to cheat as a way to attain a degree. While Dante is successful in using facts and personal examples as evidence and appealing to logos and pathos through rhetorical methods to convincingly shape his argument that the higher educational system is flawed in its policies, he is ineffective in fully appealing to ethos due to his egotistical tone throughout his paper and the unethical nature of his job.

Dante's use of fact throughout his paper serves to create compelling evidence to support his central argument. Dante uses specific numbers to describe various aspects of his job. To convey how much Dante writes in a year, he says, "In the past year, I've written over 5,000 pages of scholarly literature, most on very tight deadlines" (1). This fact shows the magnitude of cheating present in the educational system because writing 5,000 pages within just one year is too large to be attributed to the cheating of only one student. Dante's use of fact shows how prevalent the cheating problem is, which helps support his central argument about how colleges are not adequately assisting their students.

Another fact Dante uses to show the magnitude of the college cheating problem is the number of assignments he works on per day. Dante says, "Any day of the academic year, I am working on upward of 20 assignments" (2). Having more 20 assignments to complete in a single day alone is both daunting and excessive, so this fact serves to create a compelling argument about the magnitude of cheating students. Since the number of assignments to work on in a single day is so large, the use of this fact serves to show the size of the educational failure Dante discusses throughout his paper and supports Dante's argument about how problematic this failure truly is.

In addition to facts, Dante uses personal examples as evidence to support his thesis. Dante's personal examples are primarily used to provoke strong emotions from the readers so that they may understand the consequences of the educational system failure he addresses throughout his paper. One instance of a personal example from Dante that evokes strong emotions is, "I live well on the desperation, misery, and incompetence that your educational system has created" (2). This personal example evokes emotion because it uses words that are commonly associated with strong negative emotions. By using strong negative words, such as "desperation, misery, and incompetence" to describe the products of the educational system, Dante highlights the immense struggles students face. This emotional spotlight serves to further support his main thesis about the failures of the educational system to adequately assist its students.

In terms of rhetorical methods present in the paper, Dante primarily uses logos and pathos to appeal to his audience. To appeal to logos, Dante uses facts and statistics to convey evidence that is both relevant and verifiable. An example of this is evident when Dante talks about cheating within education and says, "Last summer *The New York Times* reported that 61 percent of undergraduates have admitted to some form of cheating on assignments and exams" (3). This statistic is verifiable since it is cited by a major newspaper and relevant to his main point because it shows the magnitude of the cheating problem he is addressing. Dante is able to persuade the audience through reason by using a strong, verifiable statistic, which enhances his appeal to logos.

To handle differing perspectives that may be present within his audience and therefore strengthen his appeal to logos, Dante uses anecdotes. For example, Dante describes an actual assignment he wrote for a business student, and says, "It is late in the semester when the business student contacts me, a time when I typically juggle deadlines and push out 20 to 40 pages a day" (3). This anecdote handles differing perspectives from those who believe that the college cheating problem is not a substantial issue because it shows how busy Dante's business becomes at the close of a semester. This effectively handles the perspectives of skeptics who don't see Dante's central argument as a large problem because it shows the magnitude of papers Dante must write within a day, which allows the audience to picture how much cheating occurs within the course of an academic year.

Dante also uses pathos as a rhetorical method to connect to the audience's emotions, values, and beliefs. Dante compellingly appeals to pathos when he discusses the work, he completes for seminary students and creates a stark contrast to the values of the profession and the cheating students of this profession undertake. When discussing these students, Dante says, "They seem so blissfully unaware of the inherent contraction in paying somebody to help them cheat in courses that are largely about walking in the light of God and providing an ethical model for others to follow" (5). This recollection appeals to the audience's values, since cheating directly contradicts the values of ethics commonly associated with seminary students. Using seminary students as an example creates a shock factor within the paper, which in turn magnifies Dante's appeal to pathos.

In terms of forming a bond with his audience through his appeal to pathos, Dante does not identify with college professors. Instead, he sees professors as the primary reason why he is employed as a ghostwriter. When reflecting on his own experiences in college, Dante says, "Here I was, begging anybody in authority to take my work seriously" (8). Dante alienates himself from college professors by showing a divide between his goals and those of professors. Rather, readers view Dante as a product of the educational system because he turned to helping others cheat to achieve a value that his university did not support.

While he attempts to appeal to ethos by appearing informed, Dante's overall appeal is flawed. To appear informed, Dante uses detailed examples of the pieces he has written for students, which shows how he is very well-versed in the problem he is describing. Due to his use of specific examples, Dante appears to be trustworthy; however, this trustworthiness is clouded by Dante's exaggerations of his writing ability throughout the paper and the unethical nature of his job. For example, Dante exaggerates his writing ability when he says, "I've written essays that could be adapted into Meryl Streep movies" (5). This statement shows overconfidence on Dante's part because the caliber of content in Meryl Streep movies is very high. While Dante feels as though he is a solution to the problem he is describing, he is actually a contributing factor because the students he helps aren't really learning how to be better writers. He is a capitalist and taking advantage of an opportunity to make money. Dante's role as a cheating enabler and his overall arrogance damage his appeal to the audience's sense of ethics.

Overall, Dante is successful in conveying his point of how the education system is failing students and is forcing them to cheat. He shifts the blame from himself to the higher education system because he claims the education system drives students to cheat. Dante is calling to change the education system so that it focuses on student improvement rather than grades. Ed Dante's article "The Shadow Scholar" uses his personal experience as a ghostwriter to reflect on the education system and to call for change to benefit struggling students.

Argument

What It Means to Represent Transgender Identities on Television

Nicole Gonzalez, Writing 110

For the past decade, members of the LGBTQ are being represented more than ever in mainstream media like television. There has been a significant correlation in the increase of LGBTQ representation and LGBTQ acceptance in our society. More people, whether they identify as part of this community or not, have been more open-minded and accept people with different sexualities and genders. As our society becomes more tolerant, it provides a space for people to express their sexual and gender identities more freely. In a recent study by Gallup (a company that develops public opinion polls), it showed that as of 2021, 5.6% of Americans identify as LGBTQ compared to the 3.5% in 2012.

Every year, we see more and more representation from this community as they are finally being given a spotlight in popular media like shows, movies, and music. Before, queer topics couldn't be brought up as openly as they are now because they were seen as taboo. Now, queer topics can be talked about like it's the norm, which is how it should be. According to GLAAD's (Gay & Lesbian Allegiance Against Defamation) "Where We Are on TV" report (2020), 10.2% of regular characters on television identify as LGBTQ in 2019-2020. It was recorded as the highest percentage of representation for the LGBTQ+ community as of today. This is a massive jump from where it used to be. In 2005-2006, there was less than 2% of LGBTQ+ representation on TV. We also have more queer musical artists in the top music charts like Lil Nas X, an openly gay multiplatinum singer and rapper, who has recently released an album about his life and what it's like to be queer in the music industry. His most recent trending music video depicted him having romantic and sexual relations with a male football player for his song "That's What I Want," with over 55 million views on YouTube. The ability to release a music video like that without backlash from the majority of the media is significantly different to how it was in the 80's. When Queen, the rock band, released their music video for "I Want To Break Free," their music video was banned in North America by MTV because they were dressed in drag. Queer content is widely more accepted in today's society than it has been in the past couple of decades.

Presenting LGBTQ+ content in popular media is important for our culture because it gives a voice to the people who have been prejudiced and discriminated against for centuries. A recent study by Fandom.com (2020) found that audiences are using entertainment as a way to connect with other people. Representing the LGBTQ+ community in popular media allows people to understand themselves and others, which creates a positive impact in how people interact in our society. According to UCLA's Williams Institute (Flores, 2021), 131 out of the 174 countries they have studied have experienced increased acceptance of LGBTQ+ people since 1981. The remaining countries either faced a decline or remained the same. The year 1981 is significant because that was the year when the first cases of AIDS began to appear in the U.S. When people discovered that the majority of AIDS cases were gay or bisexual men, there was strong sense of homophobia in the country. President Ronald Reagan's administration remained quiet and provided little to no funding towards AIDS relief, costing the lives of thousands of Americans. Reagan's advisor at the time even called the epidemic as "nature's revenge on gay men" (White, 2004). Most of the homophobia towards victims and members of the LGBTQ+ community at the time stemmed from the fact that there wasn't enough information that would help people understand what it was. This fear caused people to look at AIDS as a "gay disease" and alienated queer people. Fortunately, we now have more research studies and medications that help those who are affected.

It's exciting that the LGBTQ+ community has been steadily getting more representation on TV over the years. Gay and lesbian characters are now regularly appearing on shows and movies. Transgender identities are regularly being shown on television as well, however, it is not as frequent as gays and lesbians. Even though they've been around for centuries, there still seems to be issues with getting realistic depictions of these gender identities that don't involve harmful stereotypes. Another problem is that when there are shows or movies that involve a transgender character, the role is usually given to cisgender actor. Even if the actor has good intentions, this still causes a problem with misrepresentation for the community.

While there has been a rise in transgender representation in popular media, transgender identities are still being underrepresented compared to gays and lesbians on television. The other problem is that they're also being misrepresented when transgender characters are written based on stigmatizing stereotypes. If you're looking for good transgender content in shows or movies from the past two decades, there isn't a very long list. Positive representations for this community have come a long way, but there's still a history of the negative representations that they've had to endure that are still out there today. Content from the early 2000's were either documentaries about the transgender community or media that contained offensive content against trans people. In GLAAD's 2002 television report, 54% of the 102 episodes that included transgender characters on TV were categorized as containing negative depictions. These depictions often ranged from having the transgender character be cast as victims, sex workers, murderers, or villains. In the same research study, they also found that "anti-transgender slurs, language and dialogue was present in at least 61% of the catalogued episodes and storylines." An example of this would be in an episode by the popular animated show, *The Cleveland Show*, where one of the characters projectile vomits for a long period of time after discovering that he had slept with a transgender woman. The episode also had defamatory characterizations and anti-trans language. Another show is *CSI*. One of their first reoccurring villains was a transgender serial killer who steals his dead father's identity, murders his own mother, and who later commits suicide. There's also instances where the main characters of the show would openly mock the bodies of transgender murder victims. Then there's the series, *Nip/Tuck*, where they feature a character who regrets her transition, a transgender sex worker who gets beaten, and an entire season arc dedicated to a psychotic transgender pedophile that sleeps with her own son. Depictions like these can instill harmful ideas that transgender people should be feared or that they are mentally ill.

Fortunately, we have become more progressive as a society and have reduced the amount of negative content we see now. While the steady increase and frequency in "positive" or non-offensive content of transgender on television is good, what's more important is the progress we've made in depicting them as real people. When I say real, I mean trans characters that are complex and that have depth. Characters that aren't just there for shock purposes but that provide something to the show or movie's storyline. Characters whose narratives aren't just built around discovering their identity, but about other things in the story. In FX's show, *Pose*, this was shown in all their characters.

Pose is an exemplar show that has rightfully earned the respect and adoration of the LGBTQ+ community not only for its incredible storyline and actors, but for the way they positively represented the transgender community. It is a drama series set in the 1980's that explores what life and society was like in New York when you're queer. One of the main story arcs in the show was the fight against HIV/AIDS. It provides an emotional insight into the community's history of how it affected people in the 80's, while showing the characters struggling with problems that can be seen in the present-day, such as racism and poverty. What's important about the show is that it depicts people in the LGBTQ+ community in a humane and realistic way. Transgender characters in the show are important protagonists with depth and are played by real transgender actors. Even the supporting characters play important roles that aren't just for comic relief, which we've often seen being used as a joke in previous harmful media depictions that wouldn't be socially accepted today. For example, there's Blanca Evangelista, the main protagonist who creates her own ballroom "house" to not only complete in the ballroom competitions, but to create a family of her own. She provides the guidance and support that she would've wanted when she was younger to her adopted "children." She even opens her own nail salon business after being fired from her previous job for attending a protest. We also have the eccentric Elektra Abundance, who is known for being reigning champion of New York's ballroom. She's known for being a narcissist and for making snarky remarks to other ballroom competitors that she sees as inferior. However, over the course of the show, we see her become a better person. She becomes more sympathetic and allows herself to be more vulnerable in front of her friends. Even if she sees herself as the queen, she is always willing to support her friends when they need it.

What's admirable about *Pose* is that they have increased the representation of transgender people by being responsible for 26 of the 29 transgender characters that are regularly on television, including 4 characters that are HIV or AIDS positive ("Where We on TV", 2020). The show has positively impacted its audience by giving people from the community someone they can relate to, something that makes them feel seen and heard. It has also helped fight the stigma on topics like HIV/AIDS. Even those who aren't part of the LGBTQ+ community are being educated and given an insightful look at what it's like for queer people behind the scenes.

Seeing transgender characters on television is great, but you know what's even better? Transgender characters being played by transgender actors. One of the problems in Hollywood is that many times when they're casting someone for an upcoming movie or show that has a transgender character, cisgender actors are usually the first to get considered for the role. It's not just transgender actors losing potential acting opportunities. This is happening with other sexualities and genders in the LGBTQ+ spectrum too. There's also the double standard where straight or cisgender actors are allowed to play queer roles, meanwhile, transgender actors are rarely given the chance to play a cisgender character. It's not that cisgender actors can't play queer roles, it's more about authenticity. No one truly knows what it's like to be transgender other than transgender people themselves. Giving cisgender actors these roles may exacerbate the harmful stigma that transgender people aren't real and that they're just people that are crossdressing or in drag. In 2018, Scarlett Johansson received backlash from the LGBTQ+ community when they announced that she would be playing the role of Dante "Tex" Gill, a trans man, in a movie called *"Rub & Tug"*. People felt that Gill would be misrepresented and were upset that another cisgender actress was taking an acting opportunity away from a potential trans actor. I believe they're right. It's sad to know that the first trans actress to play a transgender character on television (Laverne Cox) was just recently in 2017, and not earlier. Then there's MJ Rodriguez, who played the role of Blanca in *Pose*, who was the first trans actress to be nominated for an Emmy award in 2021. In *Variety Magazine*'s interview with Rodriguez, she described her nomination as something that "pushes the needle forward so much for now the door to be knocked down for so many people—whether they be male or trans female, gender nonconforming, LGBTQIA+" (Turchiano, 2021). If we continue down this route, barriers can be broken, and we can have better representation and storytelling from talented, queer actors.

Representation like this is so important because it reflects the way people outside the trans community see them and how transgender people see themselves. As of 2021, there are over 121 million American households that have a TV (Stoll, 2021), with the average person spending 3.1 hours a day watching television (Hubbard, 2021). We are constantly being exposed to media and it influences the way we see ourselves and the way we see others. TV can be a way for people to interconnect with different social groups like other ethnicities, race, culture, communities, or in this case, sexualities, and gender. Psychologically, what we see on tv can affect the way we interact with the world. In one form or another, people have a way of labeling themselves as part of a social group, whether it's something small like identifying as a fan of *Marvel* over *D.C Comics* or being a *Boston Red Sox* fan versus the *New York Yankees*. Or something bigger like being Christian versus Protestant, or American versus European. In psychology, everyone has two different categories of social groups. One is your in-group, the group that you socially identify with. The other is the out-group, the group that you don't associate yourself with. This often leads to intergroup bias, where people see their in-group as more favorable over the out-group. Sometimes it can go as far as creating rivalries, like how Democrats and Republicans see each other as political opponents. Both groups may start to display negative behaviors like discriminating against each other or thinking negative stereotypes. However, usually when the election is over, both parties can settle their differences and support the winning candidate, and in a way, become one group.

In this context, the two groups would be people who identify as part of the LGBTQ+ community and those who don't. With more exposure of this community on popular television, a bridge could be created to reduce the negative bias towards this community and be more open to their differences. Interpersonal contact can be a way to reduce prejudices and create positive attitudes. Even if the characters we see on television are fiction, there's some that have similar traits or lives to people in real life. It can significantly influence the way we perceive the people around us.

References

Adekaiyero, A. (2021, November 22). *Eddie Redmayne says 'it was a mistake' to play a trans character in 'The Danish Girl'*. Insider. Retrieved December 10, 2021, from https://www.insider.com/eddie-redmayne-says-mistake-play-trans-character-the-danish- girl-2021-11.

Ayoub, Phillip M. "How the Media Has Helped Change Public Views about Lesbian and Gay People." *Scholars Strategy Network*, 24 May 2018, https://scholars.org/contribution/how-media-has-helped-change-public-views-about-lesbian-and-gay-people.

Clifton, D. (2020, November 25). *Negative trans media depictions harm the community's mental health.* them. Retrieved December 10, 2021, from https://www.them.us/story/negative-media-depictions-trans-people-harms-communitys-mental-health.

D'Addario, D. (2019, June 21). *Trans superstar Hunter Schafer on her moment of 'euphoria'.* Variety. Retrieved December 10, 2021, from https://variety.com/2019/tv/features/hunter- schafer-hbo-euphoria-1203248330/.

Deerwater, Raina. "GLAAD's Where We Are on TV Report: Despite Tumultuous Year in Television, LGBTQ Representation Holds Steady." *GLAAD*, GLAAD, 14 Jan. 2021, https://www.glaad.org/blog/glaads-where-we-are-tv-report-despite-tumultuous-year- television-lgbtq-representation-holds.

Ellis, Sarah Kate. "Procter & Gamble and GLAAD Study: Exposure to LGBTQ Representation in Media and Advertising Leads to Greater Acceptance of the LGBTQ Community." *GLAAD*, P&G, 27 May 2020, https://www.glaad.org/releases/procter-gamble-and-glaad-study-exposure-lgbtq-representation-media-and-advertising-leads.

Flores, Andrew R. "Social Acceptance of LGBTI People in 175 Countries and Locations." *Williams Institute*, The Williams Institute, 8 Nov. 2021, https://williamsinstitute.law.ucla.edu/publications/global-acceptance-index-lgbt/.

Hubbard, K. (2021, July 22). "Americans spent more time watching television during COVID . . ." U.S. News. Retrieved December 10, 2021, from https://www.

usnews.com/news/best-states/articles/2021-07-22/americans-spent-more-
time-watching-television-during-covid- 19-than-working.

Hughto, J. M. W., Pletta, D., Gordon, L., Cahill, S., Mimiaga, M. J., & Reisner, S. L.
(2021, January 12). *Negative transgender-related media messages are associated with
adverse mental health outcomes in a Multistate Study of Transgender Adults.* LGBT
health. Retrieved December 10, 2021, from https://www.ncbi.nlm.nih.gov/
pmc/articles/PMC7826438/.

Kane, M. (2014, December 8). *GLAAD examines ten years of transgender images
on television; more than half were negative or defamatory.* GLAAD. Retrieved
December 10, 2021, from https://www.glaad.org/blog/glaad-examines-ten-
years-transgender-images-television-more-half-were-negative-or-defamatory.

Kelsey-Sugg, A. (2018, August 16). *Psychopaths, suicidal or comic relief: Problems
with trans roles go beyond Scarlett Johansson.* ABC News. Retrieved December
10, 2021, from https://www.abc.net.au/news/2018-08-16/changing-media-
representations-of-trans- people/10114402.

Lil Nas X. "Lil Nas X - Thats What I Want (Official Video) - YouTube." *YouTube*, 17
Sept. 2021, https://www.youtube.com/watch?v=QDYDRA5JPLE.

Mocarski, R., King, R., Butler, S., Holt, N. R., Huit, T. Z., Hope, D. A., Meyer, H.
M., & Woodruff, N. (2019, October 2). *The rise of transgender and gender diverse
representation in the media: Impacts on the population.* Communication, culture &
critique. Retrieved December 10, 2021, from https://www.ncbi.nlm.nih.gov/
pmc/articles/PMC6824534/.

Official, Queen. "Queen - I Want To Break Free (Official Video)." *YouTube*, 1 Sept.
2008, Queen - I Want To Break Free (Official Video)

Oliver, D. (2020, November 27). *Hollywood's casting dilemma: Should straight, cis-gender actors play LGBTQ characters?* USA Today. Retrieved December 10, 2021, from https://www.usatoday.com/story/entertainment/celebrities/2020/11/24/should-straight-cisgender-actors-play-lgbtq-characters-in-hollywood/6327858002/.

Stoll, J. (2021, July 13). *TV households in U.S.* Statista. Retrieved December 10, 2021, from https://www.statista.com/statistics/243789/number-of-tv-households-in-the-us/.

Talusan, M. (2018, July 4). *Why Scarlett Johansson - or any CIS actor - should never play trans roles.* them. Retrieved December 10, 2021, from https://www.them.us/story/why-scarlett-johansson-or-any-cis-actor-should-never-play-trans-roles.

Theodore. "Outgroup Bias (Definition + Examples)." *Practical Psychology,* Practical Psychology, 25 Oct. 2021, https://practicalpie.com/outgroup-bias-definition-examples/.

Turchiano, D. (2021, July 13). *MJ Rodriguez becomes first trans woman up for major acting Emmy.* Variety. Retrieved December 10, 2021, from https://variety.com/2021/tv/news/mj-rodriguez-first-trans-woman-lead-acting-emmy-1235014189/.

Volsky, I. (2004, June 8). *Recalling Ronald Reagan's LGBT legacy ahead of the GOP presidential debate.* ThinkProgress. Retrieved December 14, 2021, from https://archive.thinkprogress.org/recalling-ronald-reagans-lgbt-legacy-ahead-of-the-gop- presidential-debate-a687b80d679b/.

"Where We Are on TV Report: 2005–2006 Season." *GLAAD,* GLAAD, 11 Oct. 2018, https://www.glaad.org/publications/tvreport05.

More than Role-Playing: A Virtual World

Victor Setaro, Writing 110

No matter age, gender, or location, the video game demographic is expanding exponentially, with many new gamers finding their passion during quarantines imposed by the coronavirus pandemic. Such a rampant rise has led many to wonder whether this medium of interacting with others is a healthy one. Unfortunately, the United States is also experiencing a worrying surge in gun violence, especially at schools. The suspect correlation between the two has led many well-intentioned people to question whether violent video games contribute to gun violence. Others, however, have spun negative stories about video games to generate clicks for their poorly researched articles. Despite the abundance of these pessimistic narratives, video games offer many positive benefits to society. For some, the usage of video games can be a stress reliever. For others, researchers have noted that regular users of video games scored higher on cognitive tests than those who do not actively play video games. For others still, usage of video games is a social outlet. As far as these negative narratives are concerned, one must consider that correlation does not always indicate causation. Further research is needed to establish an indisputable link relating video game usage to aggressive tendencies. Until then, though the mainstream media will continue to use video games as a scapegoat to rationalize acts of violence, the benefits of video games undoubtedly outweigh any weak correlation with increased aggressive behavior.

It should come as no surprise to anyone who has followed the news for the past decade that mainstream media promotes exaggerated, false narratives about video games being the sole root cause of aggressive behavior among teenagers. Understanding this phenomenon requires critical knowledge of the business model these organizations follow. The first order of business for news outlets is to generate a profit, *not* to report unbiased news. Studies have shown it is demonstrably true that stories that cause scaremongering garner more clicks (Copenhaver). Indeed, viewers are far more interested in reading about how video games ruin society than how they benefit socially awkward teenagers. According to David L. Altheide, "analysis suggests that this use of fear is consistent with popular culture oriented to pursuing a 'problem frame' and entertainment formats, which also have social implications for social policy and reliance on formal agents of social control." Altheide, an experienced sociologist who taught at Arizona State University for nearly forty years, suggests that the tendency for broadcasters to try to make news entertaining might also be part of the problem here. He briefly touches on the implications of this phenomenon, even using the insidious words "social control." Altheide believes the future consequences of this so-called "social control" of the media could prove far more damaging to society than temporarily tarnishing the reputation of video games. The use of fear is not at all a new tactic that these corporations are employing to entice readers to choose their article. For better or for worse, technological advancements have allowed society to move on from the days of tuning in to the evening news with Walter Cronkite to get the latest scoop. There now exists, perhaps even to a fault, a variety of news sources from which one can choose to receive their desired dose of topical event coverage. However, this presents a unique problem for broadcasting corporations: capturing the attention of a generation whose attention span does not last for very long. Indeed, the practice of exaggerating headlines has become so widespread that it now has a name: clickbait. Fear is only one of the many tools in a corporation's toolkit to drive traffic to their articles. Unfortunately, many news outlets have abused the practice, thus spawning hordes of disinformation that now makes its rounds about the Internet like a parasite.

However, the buck does not stop with powerful news corporations. Some of the onus is on the scholars that willfully choose to publish exaggerated or methodologically flawed studies. While one might wish to think that scholarly articles are the pinnacle of unbiased sources, it is vital to remember that no human author can be without bias. Furthermore, the relationship authors share with the media is often symbiotic. When a news outlet references a source, that often drives traffic to the original article; likewise, broadcasters could not operate without sourcing the material they are presenting to their audience. While this is not inherently bad, it becomes a problem when authors adopt the same tendencies of media organizations to center their articles around a false narrative, namely one that invokes fear. According to Allen Copenhaver, a professor of criminal justice at Lindsey Wilson College, "findings suggest that negative effects of violent video games exposure in children and adolescents, rather than large effect size or high methodological quality, increase the likelihood of a study being cited in other academic publications and subsequently receiving news media coverage." Altheide's revelation that media sources lean toward publishing negative narratives to generate fear is not surprising; however, Copenhaver's data revealing that even scholarly sources almost exclusively cite negative findings is much more shocking. One might ponder whether subsequent media coverage these articles receive contributes to the author's decision to cite negative studies. Regardless, humans tend to gravitate toward media which incites fear. One may even reasonably assume that many news watchers are parents seeking information on how to raise their children. With the number of child video game players on the rise, it is not much of a stretch to assume that many parents want to know the truth about whether violent video games are destructive. However, despite the reason viewers gravitate toward these stories, the data is clear: fear sells. So long as that continues to be the case, news organizations will continue to promote these less than truthful narratives surrounding video game usage.

Even those who do not subscribe to the narrative that video games are poisoning the minds of young children often do not realize the many benefits that virtual worlds offer to their consumers. Researchers have documented many psychological benefits of using video games as a teenager, one of which is improved cognitive abilities. Many people know that solving crossword puzzles or word searches can help keep cognition sharp, but it is lesser known that solving the challenges or tasks in video games can have a similar effect. Walter R. Boot, associate professor of psychology at Florida State University, asserts that "frequent action video game players often outperform non- gamers on measures of perception and cognition, and some studies find that video game practice enhances those abilities." Lots of the controversy around video games stems from the thought that there is no reason to prefer them over traditional games. However, contrary to popular opinion, these findings suggest that video games offer many benefits that even old-school games do not. These effects are likely due to the revolutionary immersive role-playing component of most popular video games. Though the concept of immersive role-playing is not new, technology has enhanced it through mediums such as video games.

Another beneficial aspect of video games is the facilitation of positive social interaction for socially awkward individuals. According to the National Institute of Mental Health, about one out of every ten children struggle with social anxiety disorder, the irrational fear of social situations. Children who develop this so-called "social phobia" tend to prefer isolated activities. However, the presumption that video gaming is an isolated activity is a gross misconception. While video games may have once been a one-player activity or used to require multiple players to be together physically, connected to the same console, this is no longer the case. The Internet is a powerful tool, which video game developers have thoroughly used to their advantage. Most games now include some social component, if not a full-blown in-game chat or voice channel. These developments are exciting for teens who struggle with social anxiety disorder. Virtual chats have proven to be an alternative for people who fear real-world social interactions with others. According to John A. Velez, assistant professor at Indiana University, "playing with a helpful teammate confirmed expectations of in-group members to reciprocate pro-social behaviors and led to increases in pro-social behaviors between teammates." Velez has conducted extensive research on the impact of video games on mental health with his graduate students. While many opponents of video game usage among youth choose to omit these beneficial effects from their conclusions, it is only fair that they are acknowledged so that both sides receive adequate representation. When considering these beneficial effects, it becomes evident that the benefits of video game usage outweigh any slim potential for an increase in aggressive tendencies, if one exists at all.

While some studies have found a weak correlation among video game users with aggressive behavior, the results are not sufficient to prove causation because they fail to eliminate other factors which might have contributed to the findings. One of the most basic tenets of psychology is that many correlations exist, but not all prove causation. The term *correlation* refers to the perceived relationship between two trends. While correlations can be a strong indicator of *causation*, they can also indicate nothing. One famous correlation which demonstrates this principle is the relation of ice cream consumption to murder rates. Studies have shown that as the rate of ice cream consumption increases, so do murder rates. It would be absurd to assert that eating ice cream causes murders, yet people continue to treat the weak correlation relating video game usage to gun violence as absolute fact. According to Dr. Agne Suziedelyte, an Economics graduate who studies the effects of media on health, there exists "no evidence that child reported violence against other people increases after a new violent video game is released. Thus, policies that place restrictions on video game sales to minors are unlikely to reduce violence." Note that Dr. Suziedelyte touches on an important point here: evidence. Establishing causation requires a controlled study that eliminates any other potential outside factors. Few studies assert that *no* correlation relates video game usage to violent behavior; however, studies do assert that without a controlled experiment, these correlations are no more valid than one which associates ice cream consumption with murder.

One must consider alternative factors which may influence the findings of studies that suggest violent video games predispose their userbase to aggressive behavior. One of the reasons that proving causation requires a controlled experiment is to ensure that any outside factors that could influence the results are not present. Since there is an abundance of factors that could induce aggressive tendencies, it is not only unfair, but it does society a great disservice to assign sole blame to video games. According to Andrew K. Przybylski, Director of Research at the Oxford Internet Institute, "[more studies] could provide a context to understand gaming effects set against a rich data milieu, including information on objective gaming behaviors, social, familial, school, individual and genetic level factors." Indeed, researchers must conduct more studies to rule out other variables before any of these popular negative narratives about video games become factual. Until then, it must be acknowledged, especially by members of the mainstream media, that such findings are nothing more than unproven correlations which have yet to be supported by data.

The world that many modern parents were born into decades ago no longer exists. The world is now digital, leading many researchers to examine the effect that new technology, such as video games, has on children just coming of age. While it is a noble effort to study these effects, researchers must conduct their studies with care. When done improperly, it only hurts the community at large. Unfortunately, one consequence of this new digital age is that it has become absurdly easy to swindle regular people over the Internet. After all, it is a modality unlike any other. So much more can be communicated over the rich formats of the World Wide Web than any other media that existed before it. However, with great power comes great responsibility. It is the onus of the researcher to study all positions on a controversial topic. As responsible citizens, we must fight against disinformation spread across social media, be it exaggerated falsehoods about video games or another issue entirely; standing by while false information runs rampant is nearly as bad as creating it.

Works Cited

Altheide, David L., and R. Sam Michalowski. "Fear in the News: A Discourse of Control." The Sociological Quarterly, vol. 40, no. 3, Informa UK Limited, Aug. 1999, pp. 475–503. Crossref, doi:10.1111/j.1533-8525.1999.tb01730.x.

Boot, Walter R., et al. "Do Action Video Games Improve Perception and Cognition?" Frontiers in Psychology, vol. 2, Frontiers Media SA, 2011. Crossref, doi:10.3389/fpsyg.2011.00226.

Copenhaver, Allen, et al. "For Video Games, Bad News Is Good News: News Reporting of Violent Video Game Studies." Cyberpsychology, Behavior, and Social Networking, vol. 20, no. 12, Mary Ann Liebert Inc, Dec. 2017, pp. 735–739. Crossref, doi:10.1089/cyber.2017.0364.

Przybylski, Andrew K., and Netta Weinstein. "Violent Video Game Engagement Is Not Associated with Adolescents' Aggressive Behaviour: Evidence from a Registered Report." Royal Society Open Science, vol. 6, no. 2, The Royal Society, Feb. 2019, p. 171474. Crossref, doi:10.1098/rsos.171474.

Suziedelyte, Agne. "Is It Only a Game? Video Games and Violence." Journal of Economic Behavior & Organization, vol. 188, Elsevier BV, Aug. 2021, pp. 105–125. Crossref, doi:10.1016/j.jebo.2021.05.014.

Velez, John A. "Extending the Theory of Bounded Generalized Reciprocity: An Explanation of the Social Benefits of Cooperative Video Game Play." Computers in Human Behavior, vol. 48, Elsevier BV, July 2015, pp. 481–491. Crossref, doi:10.1016/j.chb.2015.02.015.

Leaving Afghanistan: A Justified End

Aaron Saindon, Writing 110

"On Aug. 1, 2009, while on one of those missions, Private Fitzgibbon stepped on a metal plate wired to a bomb buried in the sunbaked earth. The blue sky turned brown with dust. The explosion instantly killed Private Fitzgibbon, 19, of Knoxville, Tenn., and Cpl. Jonathan M. Walls, a 27-year-old father from Colorado Springs. An hour later, a third soldier who was helping secure the area, Pfc. Richard K. Jones, 21, of Roxboro, N.C., died from another hidden bomb. The two blasts wounded at least 10 other soldiers" ("Grim Milestone" 1). The tragic loss of American life in Afghanistan has been going on far too long, with the conflict now reaching its 20th anniversary. It is time to put a stop to the American fatalities. While the United States has invested countless dollars and far too many lives on the war in Afghanistan, these resources have seemingly been in vain as the Afghan people continually struggle to bolster a strong central government capable of providing fi:eedom to their people independently. "On Tuesday [in 2010], the toll of American dead in Afghanistan passed 1,000, after a suicide bomb in Kabul killed at least five United States service members. Having taken nearly seven years to reach the first 500 dead, the war killed the second 500 in fewer than two. A resurgent Taliban active in almost every province, a weak central government incapable of protecting its people and a larger number of American troops in harm's way all contributed to the accelerating pace of death" ("Grim Milestone" I). As American losses of all kinds continued after 2010 our course of action proved to be erroneous and our period of effectiveness in Afghanistan had concluded. These descriptions and statistics clearly portray that the United States was correct in withdrawing our troops from Afghanistan.

Opponents to this viewpoint have several arguments. First, they claim that withdrawing entirely was inappropriate and furthermore that doing so on a publicly announced schedule was needlessly harmful and gave the Taliban an immediate advantage. As Gearan mentions: "Since it became public Tuesday, Biden's decision has been criticized by many Republicans, who called it reckless or shortsighted. Pulling out U.S. troops, and announcing the specific timetable for doing so, will lead to victories by the Taliban and more terrorist acts, they warned" (1). Next, they argue that it is the responsibility of the United States to ensure the Afghan government does not collapse at any cost in order to deny the Taliban and its potential allies the ability to gain a strong foothold. As discussed in *the* article *Afghanistan War*: "At the very least, critics of withdrawal maintain, the United States must continue to provide Afghan forces enough intelligence and military support to prevent the Taliban from completely taking control of the countty, a disaster that would have humanitarian, regional, and global repercussions. 'An American priority must be preventing the collapse of the Afghan government, lest the Taliban's partners, including al Qaeda and other jihadist terrorists, re-establish a base to plan, prepare and direct attacks against the U.S., its allies and others who don't conform to their perverted interpretation of Islam,' H.R. McMaster, a retired U.S. Almy lieutenant general who served as a national security adviser to President Trump, and Bradley Bowman, senior director of the Hoover Institution, a think tank, wrote in the *Wall Street Journal* in July 2021" (1). Finally, they maintain that the Taliban, if in control, cannot be trusted to combat terrorist groups such as Al Qaeda in Afghanistan. Highlighted here in the article *Afghanistan War:* "The Taliban, opponents assert, cannot be trusted to keep Al Qaeda or other extremist groups out of Afghanistan. 'The idea that the U.S. can leave if the Taliban promise to combat rather than conspire with these groups is . . . wrongheaded,' retired U.S. Anny general David Petraeus, who oversaw military operations in Afghanistan from July 2010 to July 2011, and Vance Serchuk, an adjunct senior fellow at the Center for a New American Security, a think tank, wrote in the *Wall Street Journal* in 2019" (1). The opposition claims that due to the reasons mentioned above we should continue to maintain a military presence in Afghanistan.

One reason lhe United States of America was conect in withdrawing our troops from Afghanistan is because their removal was a positive decision that will shift our country's attention to internal growth. As Gearan and others mention: "Biden did not declare a military victory, saying instead that a perpetual presence in the country would not serve U.S. interests. America must focus on a modern landscape of threats that is far different from that of nearly two decades ago, when the war began in response to the terrorist attacks of Sept. 11, 2001, Biden said. 'I'm now the fourth United States president to preside over American troop presence in Afghanistan. Two Republicans, two Democrats,' Biden said. 'I will not pass this responsibility on to a fifth.'. . . 'I've concluded that it's time to end America's longest war. It's time for American troops to come home,' he said . . . In his remarks, Biden said that each president who has dealt with the war has given a version of the same rationale for continuing to fight it. 'The main argument for staying longer is what each of my three predecessors have grappled with: No one wants to say that we should be in Afghanistan forever, but they insist now is not the right moment to leave,' he said" (1). Gearan and others are saying that over the last 20 years the international stage has changed drastically, and the wisest move is not for us to continue to remain in Afghanistan in a physical capacity. Touching on the idea that leaders of this country from both sides have had the opportunity to handle this complex issue in their own way and potentially find a permanent solution and so far, have not been able to, bringing our current leader to strongly state that our time to leave has arrived. Struye de Swielande continues: "It is unlikely that a Biden presidency would send large military contingents back to conflictual regions without any provocation or direct stake for the United States. Biden shares with Obama and Trump the idea of putting an end to endless wars with the withdrawal of soldiers from Syria, Iraq, and Afghanistan. Reducing the American military footprint in the world can prevent getting entangled in peripheral crises that would require boots on the ground at high cost and that would endanger the economic recovery" (Struye de Swielande, Tanguy, 6). This is relevant because it highlights the notion that these open-ended conflicts that began in the early 2000's are now coming to a close as America withdraws troops and reduces our military footprint in order to lower our 'entanglements' that can deal striking blows both in loss of life and financially. We are now beginning to look inward and put our economic success higher on the priority list. Lastly, Struye de Swielande states: "The all-out promotion of democracy and human rights since the 1990s has been characterized by numerous failures: the Rwanda genocide; wars in Somalia, Iraq, Afghanistan, and Libya; and the non-integration of Russia and China into the Western liberal order, to name but a few. Confidence in this order has collapsed, leaving the world in systemic chaos and ushering in a leadership vacuum and a crisis of legitimacy against the organizing principles of the order. In short, we are entering a period of rupture with the international order. Two possibilities can be delineated in such a context. The first possible path is to maintain the current course, continuing the head-in-the-sand policy that has characterized the United States and, even more so, Europe for several years, as these two poles of power have avoided acknowledging and adapting to new geopolitical realities and changes in the balance of power. The second possibility is to recognize this period of rupture as an opportunity, inspired by Schumpeter's (1962) process of creative destruction. This process consists in substituting an old dysfunctional model with a new, more efficient dynamic; it would make it possible to think and shape international relations from a balanced and realistic angle, as is increasingly acknowledged" (Struye de Swielande, Tanguy, 11-12). As discussed above, the long beloved American mission of promoting and delivering democracy around the world has left us over extended and shuffling resources out of the door that could be sorely used at home in important domestic matters as opposed to international conflict. Our 'head-in-the-sand' approach has seen countless resources and lives traded for very little permanent return. This withdrawal and dramatic variation from the norm of the last 20 years may be our new leadership attempting to embrace the idea mentioned of a 'period of rupture' becoming an opportunity to realign with the present times. Bringing new priorities and realistic expectations to international relations and turning our previous approach on its head entirely. Cumulatively these points all speak to the idea that putting an end to our physical presence in Afghanistan has the potential to launch America into a new era of international relations aad allow our focus to shift onward to economic growth at home.

Another reason the United States was correct in withdrawing our troops from Afghanistan was that our military had accomplished their original mission, aad it became clear that forcing democracy was not an obtainable objective. As Zucchino states: "In mid-April, President Joe Biden, declaring that the United States had long ago accomplished its mission of denying terrorists a safe haven in Afghanistan, announced that all U.S. troops would leave the country by Sept. 11. Biden said that after nearly 20 years of war, it was clear that the U.S. military could not transform Afghanistan into a modern, stable democracy. Responding in July to critics of the withdrawal, the president asked: 'Let me ask those who wanted us to stay: How many more? How many thousands more of America's daughters and sons are you willing to risk?'" (1). It is brought to light here that if American lives are going to be put on the line there must be a strong and very clear why. As President Biden said we cannot continue to write a blank check to Afghanistan when we have on many levels accomplished our original combat goal of not allowing the country to be a 'safe haven' for these terrorist groups in the area. It had become strikingly obvious that a strong democracy was not going to take root in the country despite our best efforts over nearly two decades, this goal was far beyond our reach. Bokat-Lindell and Spencer add: "Nearly two decades later, Peter Beinart argues in *The Times,* it is difficult for the United States to maintain its preferred image as a uniquely beneficent global actor. According to Brown University's Watson Institute for International and Public Affairs, post-Sept. 11 wars in which 'U.S. forces have been most significantly involved' have killed over

800,000 people, displaced 37 million and cost the United States some $6.4 trillion. (For reference, that is about $1.9 trillion more than the estimated cost of completely transitioning the U.S. power grid off fossil fuels)" (1). Here we see that while the United States is surely not to blame entirely for these statistics there is no doubt that our presence contributed, most likely significantly, to them. It is apparent that in our pursuit of imposing our democratic solution on Afghanistan we have continued to cause collateral damage while suffering our own losses, and in the meantime the cumulative result of our plans has not been as intended or satisfactory. Finally, Bokat-Lindell and Spencer mention: "Last week, Biden declined a request from Haiti's acting prime minister for military support following the assassination of that country's president, Jovenel Moïse. It was a decision that some commentators took as yet another sign of America's shrinking hegemony. 'The world's policeman is officially off duty,' Max Boot wrote in *The Washington Post*. 'After the fiascos of Iraq and Afghanistan, we have lost our appetite for democracy-building abroad. Biden doesn't use the slogan 'America First,' but he shares former President Donald Trump's aversion to nation-building and desire to end 'forever wars'" (1). Bokat-Lindell and Spencer make it clear here that President Biden is showing a great reluctance to step onto the international stage and intervene in foreign affairs. Entering the conflict in Haiti in an assisting role could quickly lead to attempting to bolster their young and struggling democracy that is experiencing tunnoil following a violent assassination. It is becoming clear that there is no interest from America in this sort of activity after the failure to instate a strong democratic government in Afghanistan. All together it becomes clear that after achieving our initial goal in Afghanistan we remained in an attempt to deliver democracy that ultimately failed, and this failure has seemingly altered the course of American international relations for the foreseeable future as we attempt to understand our shortcomings and avoid similar situations.

A final reason the United States was correct in withdrawing our troops is because despite a massive investment on our part, enabling Afghans to defend their own country has proven ineffectual and no additional amount will change that outcome. As Zucchino discusses here: "Military and police units in Afghanistan have been hollowed out by desertions, low recruitment rates, poor morale, and the theft of pay and equipment by commanders. They have suffered high casualties, which U.S. commanders have said were not sustainable. Even though the United States has spent at least $4 billion a year on the Afghan military, a classified intelligence assessment presented to the Biden administration this spring said Afghanistan could fall largely under Taliban control within two to three years after the departure of international forces . The fall was much swifter than that, 'Afghanistan political leaders gave up and fled the country,' Biden said Monday, accusing the military of laying down arms after decades of U.S. training. 'If anything, the developments of the past week reinforce that ending U.S. military involvement in Afghanistan now was the right decision'" (qtd. in Zucchino 1). Zucchino is speaking on the fact that in a critical moment when a show of strength was required by Afghan military and political leadership, several high-ranking members chose to desert their country and leave those that remained disoriented and at a great disadvantage to the Taliban forces who were able to capitalize on this vulnerability. While it was expected that a few years down the line there would be a serious power struggle that may lead to the country being under Taliban control, no one expected the mass exodus of leadership that occurred. This speaks highly to tbe idea that despite the constant efforts from American forces to build a strong Afghan military force there is clearly an intangible, and possibly several, missing pieces that we cannot simply train into the population, meaning any extended presence would be continuing to mindlessly dedicate time, effort, and resources in a futile attempt to establish a democracy and a functioning, effective military in a land with no precedent for it. O'Donnell adds: "Afghan forces are struggling to man the front lines against a resurgent Taliban, in part because of untold numbers of 'ghost' troops who are paid salaries but only exist on paper. The nationwide problem has been particularly severe in the southern Helmand province, where the Taliban have seized vast tracts of territory in the 12 months since the U.S. and NATO formally ended their combat mission and switched to training and support. 'At checkpoints where 20 soldiers should be present, there are only eight or 10,' said Karim Atal, head of Helmand's provincial council. 'It's because some people are getting paid a salary but not doing the job because they are related to someone important, like a local warlord.' In some cases, the "ghosf" designation is more literal -- dead soldiers and police remain on the books, with senior police or army officials pocketing their salaries without replacing them, Atal said" (qtd. in O'Donnell 1). This quote addresses the rampant corruption present at all levels in the Afghan military. Without the support of American forces to fill the gaps and hide these inconsistencies, truly concerning behaviors are being brought to the world's attention. From troops themselves with strong family ties not being required to report, all the way to high-ranking members not reporting casualties and simply taking the pay of their deceased subordinates, the Afghan military is severely handicapping themselves in the fight against the Taliban and revealing their true shades. Those that are present and willing to sacrifice life and limb are being betrayed by those who are supposed to be next to them on the front lines and allowing the enemy to take massive swathes of territory at the same time. Finally, Zucchino points out: "In many cases, they surrendered without a fight, sometimes following the intercession of village elders sent by the Taliban. Thousands of Afghans, frightened of reprisal killings, tried on Monday to flee the country, seeking refuge at Kabul's international airport, which was held by foreign military forces trying to assist with evacuations. The Afghan government's collapse, after the United States spent billions to support it and Afghan security forces, was a violent coda to the U.S. military mission in America's longest war. That combat mission dogged four presidents, who reckoned with American casualties, a ruthless enemy and an often confounding Afghan partner" (1). The sentiment here is that the overall morale of the people is suffering from a lack of true desire to resist the Taliban, such as the village elders who have seemingly sided with the Taliban forces and served as message bearers encouraging a peaceful surrender or those that are overrun with fear of excessive violence from the Taliban and will not step up to fight. With American forces out of the country the Afghan military has seemingly fallen victim to a lack of conviction and possibly through a lack of understanding of the complex social dynamics present throughout the country or other factors we were not able to prepare them to stand independently. However, this has also demonstrated that if we could not achieve this in 20 years it is doubtful that we would ever have been able to. Through these points it is apparent that although we have committed an overwhelming amount of resources, time, and human lives in order to try and cultivate a government and military capable of resisting the Taliban and defending their own country, the components that are lacking cannot simply be acquired through the various methods that we have employed over the last 20 years, making the present as good a time as there ever will be to withdraw our troops.

As discussed in these arguments, the United States was correct in withdrawing its military from Afghanistan. While the opposition claims that the information on the withdrawal plan was too public, that we needed to maintain a presence to ensure the Afghan government did not fall, and that we should not have trusted the Taliban to not allow terrorist groups to take haven in the country, these arguments are not strong enough to rationalize our physical presence in Afghanistan. First, we were correct in withdrawing because the removal of our forces will allow us to dedicate more resources and attention domestically instead of sending them overseas to serve a 20 year war that could have been continued for another 20 years easily. Furthennore, we were justified because we had accomplished our original mission of denying terrorist organizations easily accessible safe havens in Afghanistan, while our secondary goal of establishing a strong democracy was revealed to be no longer feasible. Finally, the decision was proper because after endless investments, the Afghan people still appear to be ultimately unwilling to sustain their own freedom and have created several obstacles that any continuing military support from America would only delay and never fully resolve in any pennanent capacity. As expressed throughout these arguments, while the situation in Afghanistan is far from resolved, our role and contributions have gone far enough, and often without comparable return from the Afghan people, to justify our withdrawal. Our desired plan for the country, a strong central democracy, would never become viable with the citizens of the country. Now the future lies in the hands of the remaining Afghan leaders, and we can only hope that they become revitalized and do not entirely squander the past 20 years of resources and training, and instead combat the Taliban and assemble some form of government that every man, woman, and child can feel protected, represented, and proud to be united underneath.

Works Cited

Bokat-Lindell, Spencer. "Is the United States Done Being the World's Cop?" *New York Times*, 20 Jul. 2021. https://ccsu.idm.oclc.org/login?url=https://www.proquest.com/blogs-podcasts-websites/is-united-states-done-being-world-s-cop/docview/2553351600/se-2?accountid=9970.

Gearan, Anne et al. "Biden Tells Americans 'We Cannot Continue the Cycle' in Afghanistan as He Announces Troop Withdrawal" *The Washington Post*, 14 Apr. 2021. https://ccsu.idm.oclc.org/login?url=https://www.proquest.com/blogs-podcasts-websites/biden-tellsamericans-we-cannot-continue-cycle/docview/2512593993/se-2?accountid=9970.

Struye de Swiela nde, Tanguy. "The Biden Administration: An Opportunity to Affinn a Flexible and Adaptive American World Leadership." *World Affairs*, vol. 184, no. 2, Summer 2021, pp. 130-150.

Zucchino, David. "Twenty Years, Four Presidents and a Mission that Went Awry." *New York Times*, 16 Aug. 2021. https://ccsu.idm.oclc.org/login?url=https://

www.proquest.com/newspapers/twenty-years-four-presidents-mission-that-went/docview/2561599834/se-2?accountid=9970.

"Afghanistan War: Was the United States Right to Have Withdrawn from Afghanistan" *Issues & Controversies,* Infobase, 31 Aug. 2021, icof.infobase.com/articles/QXJ0aWNsZVRleHQ6MTY1NDc=. Accessed 7 Dec. 2021.

"Grim Milestone: 1,000 Americans Dead." *New York Times,* 18 May. 2010. https://ccsu.idm.oclc.org/login'?url=https://www.proquest.com/blogs-podcasts-websites/grimmilestone-1000-americans-dead/docview/2218673592/se-2?accountid=9970.

O'Donnell, Lynne, and Mirwais Khan. "Afghan Anny's 'Ghost Soldiers'; Troops are on the Books, but Exist Only on Paper. Taliban has Taken Advantage." *Los Angeles Times,* 17 Jan. 2016. ProQuest, https://ccsu.idm.oclc.org/login?url=https://www.proquest.com/newspapers/afghanarmys-ghost-soldiers-troops-are-on-books/docview/1757498747/se 2?accountid=9970.

The United States was Wrong to Withdraw from Afghanistan

Marc Perras, Writing 110

"Al-Qaeda's strength and ability to strike the West has significantly diminished over the past decade, but its leader Ayman al-Zawahiri is believed to still be based in Afghanistan along with a number of other senior figures in the group. The Afghan intelligence services announced on Saturday they had killed Husam Abd al-Rauf, a high-ranking Egyptian al-Qaeda member, in an operation in Ghazni province. Mr. Fitton-Brown told the BBC that despite its lower profile, al-Qaeda remained 'resilient' and 'dangerous' (qtd. In "Al-Qaeda Still 'Heavily Embedded' within Taliban in Afghanistan, UN Official Warns Page 1). The United States first entered Afghanistan in 2001 with the purpose of tracking down and kill those responsible for 9/11. This turned out to be Al-Qaeda with Osama bin Laden at the forefront. Although he has been eliminated, the group itself has not. They are still active and in Afghanistan. They have been marginalized with American presence. However, what will happen now when the Taliban take over? Will they work with the existing government, or will they rule with brute force as they did in the past? Furthermore, will they allow their extremist allies to regain power in the area? As we now know, our worst fears are now manifesting, the Taliban have shown to continue to have ties to al-Qaeda. With their complete takeover of the Afghanistan government and the continual rule with an iron and brutal fist, they are permitting their extremist allies to establish havens to build their strength and plan attacks in the west. As states in "By the Numbers": "Approximate number of Afghan civilians killed in Afghanistan War 50,000" (1). While tens of thousands of Afghanis were collateral damage during the U.S. presence in Afghanistan, many more will likely suffer under the merciless rule of the Taliban. Freedom and democracy, which the U.S. had worked to establish, have come to an abrupt end, replaced with brutal punishment for minor infractions of the Taliban's interpretation of Sharia law. Together, these arguments support the conclusion that the United States should not have withdrawn its troops from Afghanistan for the safety of the Afghanistan and American people the United States should not have withdrawn from Afghanistan.

The first reason as to why the United States should have not withdrawn its military from Afghanistan is to protect the people of Afghanistan from the Taliban's unethical rule. In "Afghanistan War Was the United States Right to Have Withdrawn from Afghanistan?" it states: "The Taliban resurgence was particularly strong in Helmand, a southern province where corruption and abuse of power among administrators appointed by Karzai had fueled popular discontent. In Helmand and other provinces, the Taliban infiltrated villages, secured the loyalty of local elders, and assassinated officials or villagers with suspected allegiances to the Afghan state or ISAF" (1). This shows the basic civil liberties that are being broken Everday under Taliban rule. The people are mled with an iron fist and any that speak out are killed on the spot. This is no way for humans to live and should not be allowed to occur. A withdrawal only exemplifies these examples and every day since America left, we continue to have blood on our hands. The article also adds: "A stark rise in insurgent attacks in 2006 raised doubts that Karzai's government and international forces were capable of protecting civilians from a seemingly resurgent Taliban. That year, the number of suicide bombings and the use of improvised explosive devices (IEDs)—which blow up by remote control or upon being stepped on or driven over—skyrocketed in comparison to previous years. To carry out suicide bombings, the Taliban often recruited poor and mentally handicapped young men, as well as fighters seeking revenge for family members who had died in coalition bombings or raids. Recruits studied in Pakistani madrassas where they learned they would be rewarded in the afterlife for carrying out such attacks" (1). This quote is important because it shows the disregard of life the Taliban have. They would recruit people who are at their absolute lowest and promise them a good ending of they wear an IED and blow-up innocent civilians. They are cruel, oppressive leaders and America lets them gain control of a country with millions of innocent people. Finally, in "Al-Qaeda Still 'Heavily Embedded' within Taliban in Afghanistan, UN Officitil Warns" it states: "It is feared the Afghan peace process is in any case losing its momentum. Despite the beginning of long delayed negotiations between the Taliban and an Afghan government-led delegation last month in Qatar, violence has continued and even intensified in recent weeks. The negotiations have stalled amid attempts to resolve preliminary issues, with major issues such as a ceasefire or power-sharing arrangement yet to be discussed. There are fears that if US troops are withdrawn next year, before an agreement has been reached, the violence could intensify and the Taliban push for a military victory" (Secunder 4). This quote shows to the unwillingness of the Taliban to work towards a resolution. They are not people who can be persuaded or are ready to compromise. They want to rule the way they want, which has been proven to be an oppressive regime. The American withdrawal left a country without the means or money to defend itself from an enemy that wants nothing more than to see the people be oppressed. As these points indicate, a total withdrawal from Afghanistan is a horrible idea that will lead to a major human rights crisis which should not occur. It is America's duty to protect freedom for all and that is the exact opposite of what happened during the withdrawal. We made the conscious decision to let the Afghanistan people be oppressed.

Another reason as to why the United States should not have pulled out of Afghanistan is because a retreat would damage our reputation on the world stage. According to Lisa Curtis, the director of the indo-pacific security program states in an interview with Vox: '"The first option would be what you presented as pulling out all US troops. That would risk a civil war, the reemergence of a terrorist safe haven, and a tremendous loss of US credibility built with our allies'" (qtd. In Ward 3). This quote from Curtis explains how leaving Afghanistan has made us appear weak and disloyal. It will reduce the esteem and respect with which the United States has been regarded by many because other people around the world who rely on our aide will examine the situation that unfolded in Afghanistan and will wonder if we would treat them the same way we treated the Afghani's if we agreed to supply military assistance. This could lead to not as many people wanting to help because they will be worried that we will abandon them as we did the Afghani's. This could mean that the US is viewed more negatively throughout the world. Curtis also adds: "'Let's not forget that the US provides moral support, too. Having the US there is a source of reassurance for the Afghans. The minute the US says, "we're going to zero troops," you're going to see a lot of Afghans flee the country, you're probably going to see a refugee crisis, which the Europeans are really worried about. There are a lot of impacts that happen when the US takes that ultimate step of going to zero"' (qtd. In Ward 3). Curtis once again identifies the myriad negative consequences that could, and have, resulted from our withdrawal from Afghanistan. Our perceived betrayal of Afghanistan will mean a deluge of refugees descending on our allies in Europe. Given the large numbers who have and will seek to flee, a refugee crisis may well occur and add on to the immigration crisis currently occurring in Europe. This will not enhance our relations with our allies in Europe and elsewhere. Finally, Secunder, states in "Al-Qaeda still 'Heavily Embedded' within Taliban in Afghnaistan, UN official warns." that: "One diplomat closely observing the process told the BBC the US withdrawal plans were no longer 'condition based' but 'agenda based', suggesting President Trump's overriding priority is to end America's longest-ever war. At times President Trump has appeared out of step with military advisers, recently criticizing defense officials who, he said, 'want to do nothing but fight wars" (4). This quote demonstrates that Trump's motivations may have had nothing to do with military objectives, the welfare of the Afghans, or our national security. Rather the·priority for Trump was to secure his re-election. A withdrawal negotiated on this basis would be morally and ethically reprehensible and would damage our relations with our allies worldwide, never mind causing great harm to the people of Afghanistan. All this information points towards that a total withdrawal from Afghanistan would negatively impact our global reputation and could harm our relations with present and future allies

A final reason as to why the United States should have maintained a military presence in Afghanistan is to stop the creation of the most dangerous safe haven for extremists the world has ever seen. In "Al-Qaeda Still 'Heavily Embedded' within Taliban in Afghanistan, UN Official Warns" it states: "But Edmund Fitton-Brown, coordinator of the UN's Islamic State, Al-Qaeda and Taliban Monitoring Team, has told the BBC that the Taliban promised al-Qaeda in the run-up to the US agreement that the two groups would remain allies" (4). This is particularly important because it shows that even when the Taliban had made the deal with America on the withdrawal that they were still allied to the group responsible for 9/11. The group has already committed the worst terrorist attack in American history and now they will have free reign to regain power in the lawless Afghanistan. In "Afghanistan War Was the United States Right to Have Withdrawn from Afghanistan?" it states: "And, as we know, in 2011, America hastily and mistakenly withdrew from Iraq. As a result, our hard-won gains slipped back into the hand of terrorist enemies. Our soldiers watched as cities they had fought for, and bled to liberate, and won, were occupied by a terrorist group called ISIS. The vacuum we created by leaving too soon gave safe haven for ISIS to spread, to grow, recruit, and launch attacks. We cannot repeat in Afghanistan the mistake our leaders made in Iraq" (1). This shows that we have prior knowledge of what a hastily withdrawal could cause. The Taliban in control could lead to other extremists' groups rising to power. They could be bigger and stronger than others we have delt with in the past. This quick withdrawal could also lead the U.S. to be forced to re-enter Afghanistan to destroy a new threat. This could lead to thousands of more American deaths and the start of a new war. Finally in Curtis's Interview with Vox she says: "But remember also that if the Taliban came back to power, you'll see terrorists from all over the world—not just al Qaeda—you'll see a convergence of extremists and terrorists back in Afghanistan. It's likely to be a worse terrorist safe haven than it was before 9/11" (qtd. In Ward 3). This quote shows the frightening realization that a withdrawal could cause lots of innocent lives to be lost.

Afghanistan would become a hideout for the worst groups to ever walk this earth and there would be no one there to keep them in place. Without American forces in Afghanistan the extremists can become enormously powerful and as states even more powerful than before the 9/11 attacks which means that thousands of innocent lives are now in danger Everday. This evidence points towards that due to the American withdrawal from Afghanistan. It is now expected that extremists from all around the world will now have a location to be grow and gain power which they will then use to attack the west and all its people.

There are some arguments used by the people who think the United States were right to pull out of Afghanistan. First, they argue that The United States has spent so much tax dollars in Afghanistan already and has gotten us nowhere. As stated in "Afghanistan War": "The Costs of War, a team of scholars and legal experts, estimates that the United States has spent more than $2 trillion on military operations, aid and reconstruction efforts, and care for veterans of the conflict" (1). Second, they maintain the number of Americans killed or injured is already too high. According to "By the Numbers", approximately 2500 men and women lost their lives in Afghanistan, and thousands more were wounded (2). The Third and final argument is that we have been in Afghanistan for two decades and early on accomplished our original goal. Since then, we have invested tremendous resources in attempting to dislodge and subdue the Taliban, Without success. Our effort there had simply become a losing battle. As President Biden stated: "My fellow Americans, the war in Afghanistan is now over. I'm the fourth President who has faced the issue of whether and when to end this war. When I was running for President, I made a commitment to the American people that l would end this war. And today, I've honored that commitment. It was time to be honest with the American people again. We no longer had a clear purpose in an open ended mission in Afghanistan. After 20 years of war in Afghanistan, I refused to send another generation of America's sons and daughters to fight a war that should have ended long ago. After more than $2 trillion spent in Afghanistan—a cost that researchers at Brown University estimated would be over $300 million a day for 20 years in Afghanistan—for two decades—yes, the American people should hear this: $300 million a day for two decades . . . We've been a nation too long at war. If you're 20 years old today, you have never known an America at peace" (US gov 5). For these reasons there are many people who believe it was right to withdraw from Afghanistan.

All these reasons led to one conclusion the United States was wrong to withdraw its military from Afghanistan. Whiie the opposition will argue that we have already invested so much time and money as well as lost so many American and Afghani lives in this 20 yearlong war that a withdraw must occur, they are wrong. Because yes, a lot of money and time was spent as well as a lot of lives lost but those were invested into a prize which we cannot see which is safety. Without those continued sacrifices the United States and its allies could be in danger. First, it was wrong to pull out of Afghanistan because it is our duty as Americans to help out those in need. We should act to maintain basic human rights for all so that all humans can live their best lives. We should not let the Taliban infringe upon the Afghanistan people. In Addition, A complete withdrawal from Afghanistan will make us look bad in the eyes of the world. This could lead to some serious complications down the road especially with our allies when they are unsure if they can trnst that we will be by their side when they need us the most or we will just abandon them like we did to the Afghanistan people. Finally, the United States should not have pulled out because without our presence there and the Taliban in control Afghanistan will become a safe haven for extremist groups like Al-Qaeda which could spell disaster for the free world. These reasons show that despite, the money, time, and lives lost there is still a need for the United States to be in Afghanistan. The Afghanistan government is not ready to handle the Taliban yet and they might not be for many years, but that time would be worth the wait because this shouldn't be about some political points to cash in latter. This is about people's lives and the safety of innocent civilians and money, and time should not be more important than making sure people have the basic right to live.

Works Cited

"Afghanistan War." *Issues and Controversies*, Infobase, 31 Aug. 2021,icof.infobase. com/articles/QXJ0aWNsZVRleHQ6MTY1NDc=. Accessed 1 Nov. 2021.

"By the Numbers: Afghanistan War." *Issues and Controversies*, Infobase, 30 Aug. 2021,icof.infobase.com/articles/QXJ0aWNsZVRleHQ6MTcxMDQ=.Accessed 21 Nov. 2021.

Kennani, Secunder. "Al-Qaeda Still 'Heavily Embedded' within Taliban in Afghanistan, UN Official Warns." *BBC News,* BBC, 29 Oct. 2020, https://www. bbc.com/news/world-asia-547114525.

United States, White House. *Remarks by President Biden on the End of the War in Afghanistan.* 31 Aug. 2021, https://www.whitehouse.gov/briefing-room/ speeches-remarks/2021/08/31/remarks-by-president-biden-on-the-end-of-the-war-in-afghanistan/.

Ward, Alex. "The Best Case against Withdrawing All US Troops from Afghanistan." *Vox*, Vox, 17 Mar. 2021, https://www.vox.com/22327124/afghanistan-troop-withdrawal-biden-lisacurtis-stay.

Job Satisfaction & Happiness: A Secret Key to Economic Success

Ashton Peterson, Writing 110

If you are like almost 51% of Americans, you hate your job. 2 in 5 workers report their workload, daily stress, and poor management as factors actively contributing to a rapidly increasing population of discouraged and burnt-out employees, mostly in the youngest group of those surveyed. With the power of electricity and the rate of technological progress humanity has made, why does it feel like jobs are becoming more and more stressful? If anything, automation and the exponential growth of manufacturing potential should have made work easier—yet it seems to have had the opposite effect. In the book *The Overworked American: The Unexpected Decline of Leisure*, Juliet Schor claims that the average pre-industrial worker had a shorter work week than most Americans do today. Of course, the modern standard of living enjoyed today far outweighs that of late Medieval Europe, but this information still airs a series of key questions. What contributes to the rise of labor time, and the loss of leisure? What does this mean for the economy, and more importantly, ourselves? How can we find meaning in our workplaces? Unsurprisingly, the answer is complicated. Not only do employers have a duty to create a productive and satisfying workplace, but the employees themselves have a large impact based on their attitudes alone. Despite the historical difficulties of balancing company profit and fair employee compensation, companies need to sacrifice a bit of their bottom line, and workers must instill a meaning of their own in labor to truly reach a healthy balance between happiness and productivity.

The often-overlooked history of organized labor is a bloody and distressing one, filled with violent protests, strike-breaking, and a variety of unscrupulous tactics employed by both the company owners and its workers to force the other side into submission. In extreme cases, labor leaders were even stalked by corporate bounty hunters, and risked being seriously beaten or blackmailed for advocating workers' protections. Fortunately, key legislation in the early 1900s and continuously changing business practices have made these seemingly archaic feuds obsolete, at least in highly productive societies like the United States. Organized pushes from Unionized workers allowed for the passage of the "Fair Labor Standards Acts of 1938, which mandated a minimum wage, extra pay for overtime work, and basic child labor laws" (Investopedia). Low-skilled labor was traditionally held in surplus, and the lack of education and opportunity to unionize undermined the worker's ability to negotiate with their bosses. As machinery and groundbreaking automation transformed the workplace for millions, the dynamic of this formula of labor changed drastically. New workers and their specialist skills were no longer disposable and easily replaced; companies were now forced to come to the bargaining table. What the industrialized world has today no longer reflects a system of ultra-powerful corporations abusing their down-trodden workers; instead resembling a multi-faceted, and often mutually-beneficial relationship. Companies want to retain their workers, and the investment made in training them; workers want more pay and more freedom. But if highly trained workers have a newfound edge in negotiation, then why do so many people report frustration with their jobs?

One of the reasons is simple: their work follows them home. Although online labor advocates may propose distance working as a solution, it is instead indicative of a larger problem. The idea that working from home may alleviate some of the burden on workers does have some merit in the short run, however it is far from a feasible strategy to reduce unhappiness over extended periods of time. There are definite advantages to working online for many people, but the relatively distraction-free environment of an office can be appealing for workers and employers both. A study from the *National Bureau of Economic Research* found that although at-home workers were almost 14% more productive and 9% more engaged in their work, at the end of the study period, most at-home workers wanted to go back to the office. Despite higher job satisfaction among "at-homers," these same employees reported a higher degree of loneliness and suffered from a dearth of economic benefits in comparison to their in-office counterparts, including losses in raises and promotions. Whether at home or at work, the advent of the internet and the cellphone has created the expectation that employees should always be on call. High earners such as doctors and executives all the way down to project managers and general office workers can be pressured to be available at any time, either asked to come in on their weekends or to join a meet online. The COVID-19 pandemic has seriously exacerbated this problem, forcing employees to juggle increasingly complex schedules and workloads from home, without the benefit of face-to-face communication with their managers and peers. Increased workload often overflows into other aspects of employees' lives, making housekeeping and rest time increasingly scarce. Working at home may appear to address issues with happiness at work, but it seems it is only effective temporarily.

Trying to increase job satisfaction is not only a one-sided problem; employers benefit from workplace happiness as much as their employees do. Countless studies highlight the extreme profitability of highly satisfied workforces, citing the higher level of engagement in their work and in particular the reduced turnover rate of employees. Happy workers stay and return the company's investment in training them, while unsatisfied workers "turnover" out of the company to find new jobs. "Raises matter to Americans," writes Jack Flynn of Zippia Research, "as a considerable 54.2% of employees say they would leave their current job for a pay raise." It is distressing that many Americans report that they search for meaning in their work, but would leave their field just for the opportunity for a higher salary. This is not to say that laborers are inherently greedy, rather, people also crave respect, and it is clear that higher wages demonstrate a company's appreciation for an individual worker's effort. Salaries and wages are the largest expenses for almost all American-based companies; it makes sense that financial officers would want to reap the most benefits from their largest liability. It is within their best interest to take a temporary blow to the income of a company to possibly avoid the industry average of $550 billion dollars lost to unhappy employees annually. Dissatisfaction is also associated with a staggering 18% decrease in productivity and 15% in profitability in the aggregate (Flynn). There is a very clear, positive correlation between a worker's compensation and their satisfaction, and another upward-sloping relationship between satisfaction and productivity. Companies not only could voluntarily increase the pay of their workers to increase happiness, but there is even a basis to suggest that doing so would also improve the outcomes of the business as well.

Raising wages is not the only way that corporations can buffer low job satisfaction numbers; one of the most instrumental ways to improve workplace morale is to explicitly outline a company culture that will motivate laborers. People across the board respond to meaning— and are compelled to work harder when they believe what they are doing is important. Job satisfaction is inseparably linked to how vital workers perceive their work to be, and companies can provide a boost to happiness by simply communicating a powerful central message. "We want to do something that's bigger than ourselves and the need to earn a paycheck. Our work can give us some of that meaning when we understand the deeper why behind it," Don Shapiro writes, underlining the massive implications of something as seemingly simple as an individual's attitude. However, this problem is easier to speak to than address. In this same article focused on company culture, Shapiro reveals that less than 12% of managerial staff believe they understand company culture, despite the fact that companies with successful cultures earn 85% more on average. It cannot be understated how vital workplace happiness is, given how mutually beneficial this aspect of business is to both employers and employees. Often, this crucial relationship is overshadowed by unfounded beliefs that employee benefits are always a detriment to their company's bottom line when it is usually the other way around. By raising wages, delivering additional benefits to employees, and developing a working culture, companies can both serve their workers by creating a gratifying environment and even increase their own profitability—sometimes explosively.

However, the issue of job satisfaction does not only lie within the company's jurisdiction. Employees have an obligation to create their own happiness. In the *2018 Indian Journal of Positive Psychology*, researchers studied how people's mindsets can impact both their satisfaction and performance at work. Researchers stratified their subjects into two identifiable subgroups: one set had an Internal Locus of Control, and the other had an External Locus of Control. Individuals with internal locuses generally believe they can impact the outcomes of their life, and that their behavior has a direct connection with the results of their actions. Those with external locuses instead attribute their success and failures to cosmic forces and outside influence, such as good or bad luck. Previous studies have shown that those with internal locuses of control are more responsible, resilient, and content with life. In hindsight, it sounds obvious, but the results were very clear. "The results of correlation analysis indicate that. . . locus of control (external) is found significantly negatively correlated with satisfaction," (Singh, Singh, Gupta 71). What this means is, the study concluded that people with internal locuses benefited more from positive life events and the positive emotions correlated with them and were more resilient to the effects of negative emotions from comparatively bad life events, such as divorce and losing a loved one. When employees develop internal locuses of control, their work becomes measurably more important and more meaningful, which is directly related to their level of happiness at work and at home.

Most Americans spend 33% of their days either at work or completing job-related tasks; it is absolutely essential that this time is not gone to waste. For everyone working or managing, it is imperative that those in the workplace recognize both the necessity of a satisfied worker, both for the mental health of the individual as well as the bottom line of the company they work for. It would not be amiss to highlight the correlation between happiness and a job well done, which is ultimately the primary goal of a recruiter looking for additional help. Employers can pay their employees a bonus rate to incentivize them, and by changing their mindset and searching for what they are passionate about, employees can bolster their attitudes. There are no perfect solutions to this problem—adversity and just doing boring things are a part of any job, and unfortunately, life can sometimes be brutally disappointing. However, as researchers and even regular people just living their lives begin to chip away at this issue, extraordinary progress has been made trying to find a healthy medium to make work environments satisfying and happy for everyone.

Works Cited

Sandroff, Ronni. "The History of Unions in the United States." *Investopedia*, 8 Sept. 2021, https://www.investopedia.com/financial-edge/0113/the-history-of-unions-in-the-united-states.aspx.

Flynn, Jack. "43 Incredible Job Satisfaction Statistics [2021]: Average Job Satisfaction in the US." *Zippia*, Dec. 2021, 43 Incredible Job Satisfaction Statistics [2021]: Average Job Satisfaction In The US – Zippia.

Shapiro, Don. "Build a Company Culture That Delivers Eye-Popping Results." *Business 2 Community*, Oct. 2021. Build a Company Culture That Delivers Eye Popping Results - Business 2 Community.

Bloom, Nicholas. Liang, James. Roberts, John. Ying, Zhichun Jenny. "Does Working From Home Work? Evidence From a Chinese Experiment." *National Bureau of Economic Research*, Mar. 2013. Microsoft Word - Feb 20 (nber.org)

Singh, A. P., et al. "Role of Life Events Stress and Locus of Control (External) in Job Satisfaction: An Empirical Evidence." *Indian Journal of Positive Psychology*, vol. 9, no. 1, Jan. 2018, pp. 69–73. EBSCOhost, doi:10.15614/ijpp.v9i01.11745.

Research Report

The Academic Struggles of Living with Anxiety: A Study of the Effect of Clinical Anxiety on High School Teenagers

Erica Klem, Writing 110

Abstract

This report examines and answers the following research question: How does medically diagnosed anxiety affect the academic progress of American high school students? Investigation of this topic led to the thesis that American high school students with anxiety can experience patterns of impulsive and/or over-thinking, a lack of social skills, and an absence of appropriate treatment, which can all negatively-affect their academic progress. 2.2% of American adolescents aged 13-18 are diagnosed with Generalized Anxiety Disorder and 9.1% are diagnosed with Social Anxiety Disorder. This statistic exhibits the fact that more adolescents have anxiety than people think, so it is important to bring attention to the problems that those in an anxious state-of-mind have to deal with.

I. Purpose

This research question is important to those with medically diagnosed anxiety because people without anxiety do not completely understand what they go through. A common example of misunderstanding the hardships that come with anxiety is someone saying, "Just try not to think about it!" One may think that it is easy to deal with this condition, but there are many factors that go into the cause of someone's anxiety and many obstacles that make it harder to become less anxious. This research study will allow those who do not have medically diagnosed anxiety to learn about the day-to-day challenges, symptoms, and/or negative effects that anxious high-schoolers face when in an academic setting, and, hopefully, will raise awareness about living with this condition and how to supplement and care for those who have it.

II. Methods

The most useful article pertaining to this research was, "The Relationship between Negative Urgency and Generalized Anxiety Disorder Symptoms: the Role of Intolerance of Negative Emotions and Intolerance of Uncertainty" by Elizabeth Pawluk and Naomi Koerner. This article showed to be most useful due to the authors covering two different sides of how a person with anxiety thinks and acts. While it is fairly known that people with anxiety tend to over-think situations, the authors also mention how they can think and act impulsively because they cannot deal with their own emotions, nor uncertainty. This interesting viewpoint helps bring awareness to the troubles that high school students with medically diagnose anxiety may face because it explains their thought-process and the reasons for their actions in certain situations. In other words, the article helps those without anxiety understand what it is like to live with that disorder.

III. Findings

While high school is already known, by most, to be one of the hardest phases of life, it is even more difficult to tolerate in concurrence with a medically diagnosed anxiety disorder. Although it may go unnoticed by teachers and fellow classmates, those with anxiety are battling different circumstances every day. These circumstances, in turn, can set off many reactions that range from avoidance, to panic, to completely shutting oneself down. American high school students with anxiety can experience patterns of impulsive and/or over-thinking, a lack of social skills, and an absence of appropriate treatment, which can all negatively affect their academic progress.

There are several different forms of medically diagnosed anxiety; however, two of the most common forms are Generalized Anxiety Disorder (GAD) and Social Anxiety Disorder (SAD). According to the American Psychiatric Association, GAD is characterized as, ". . . persistent and excessive worry that interferes with daily activities," whereas SAD is characterized as, ". . . anxiety and discomfort about being embarrassed, humiliated, rejected or looked down on in social situations." To officially be diagnosed with one of these disorders, one should first have a discussion with their doctor; a doctor can help their patients work through troubling matters and provide them with the appropriate resources, such as a qualified therapist, psychologist, or even a mental-health group. Once personal situations are spoken about with a doctor, tests such as assessment measures can be carried out to diagnose the disorder, such as a severity test where questions regarding thought, feelings, and behaviors are answered by the patient or must be filled out by a clinician ("What are Anxiety Disorders?").

Anxiety is usually associated with the symptom of over-thinking situations, meaning easy tasks in school can become much harder than they are supposed to be. It is extremely difficult for someone in a state of caution to effectively evaluate benefits and drawbacks and form a valid decision. In turn, ideas can be easily misinterpreted and the wrong actions can be taken. This problem can prevent someone from growing academically as they focus too much on irrelevant details and struggle to grasp main concepts. Pawluk and Koerner of Ryerson University in Canada state, "GAD symptoms display a need to gather a large amount of information before making a decision, even when the decision is relatively inconsequential," (qtd. in Tallis et al.). With this kind of mindset, a high school student with GAD can have difficulties in classes where they must provide their own opinion or give reasons for an answer. The format of gathering information can cause them to go too far in depth and not be able to make a decision, but rather confuse themselves about the question being asked and take it too literally. Multiple choice questions can also become a nuisance because of how closely-related some answers may be. By over-thinking, students can diminish their understanding of topics and focus too little on what is really important.

Although people with GAD tend to over-think situations and make decisions too slowly, intolerance of uncertainty and of one's own negative emotions can also cause them to have impulsive thinking, leading to a reduction in positive academic performance. Since negative emotions can be unwanted but occur uncontrollably, a high school student may find it easier to completely shut down or avoid the problem as much as possible. Additionally, a high level of uncertainty can cause them to act impulsively than to deal with the problem at hand. Pawluk and Koerner say that as, ". . . their capacity for rational reasoning is diminished, their attention is directed to immediate rather than long-term consequences, and they prioritize rapid modification of their intense discomfort, even when they know these actions are likely to be counter-productive in the longer run" (611). For example, lots of high school students regularly procrastinate because they're too lazy to work on an assignment. However, a high school student with GAD would procrastinate because they cannot tolerate their emotions of worry that the assignment is too hard, will take too long, or the possibility of receiving a low grade on it. Even though the decision to procrastinate will negatively affect the quality of their assignment in the long-run, they are doing what is best for themselves in the short-run—eliminating their excessive worry.

Along with over-thinking, a lack of social skills can negatively affect a high school student's ability to participate in class. It is normal to have a small amount of fear of being embarrassed, but when a student has SAD, they will have excessive fear and try to avoid situations they deem embarrassing as much as possible. A study conducted by Mehtalia and Vankar in India showed that out of a group of 421 high school students, 54 were diagnosed with SAD (222). Among these 54 students, it was most commonly reported that, "Being criticized scares [them] a lot . . . [They are] afraid of doing things when people might be watching . . . Being embarrassed or looking stupid are among [their] worst fears . . . [They] would do anything to avoid being criticized" (Mehtalia and Vankar 223). With this type of mentality, a high school student with SAD would surely have trouble with school performance. For instance, avoiding certain situations such as class presentations or discussions would cause a decrease in one's participation grade. Choosing to not participate, such as by asking questions, would also diminish a student's understanding of class concepts because they are, now, not able to fully comprehend what is being taught, which means they will also not be able to apply that lesson to future assignments.

Even worse, the act of avoiding social situations can form a cycle that continuously damages a high school student's academic abilities. This cycle begins when the student first avoids the situations they are afraid of. In turn, their grades and knowledge are negatively-affected, which could cause them to avoid these situations even more because they do not have the experience to prepare themselves for those circumstances. Luigi Mazzone, member of the Department of Child Neurology and Psychiatry in Italy, insists that, "While poor school performance can result from excessive anxiety, it can also be itself the cause of anxiety, low self-esteem, and other affective symptoms, thus creating a self-maintaining cycle" (2). This cycle explains how a student may become trapped even further in their anxiety as it is fed exactly by what they are avoiding. Because of the continuous cycle, students will never be prepared for social interactions in school, such as working in groups, and will face more and more side-effects the longer the cycle runs for.

The greatest thing that can affect a high school student's academic achievements is not receiving the proper or appropriate amount of treatment for their anxiety. It is important for everyone, whether they have medically diagnosed anxiety or not, to keep in mind that anxiety is a real disorder that does negatively impact those who have it. Without this understanding, it can be extremely difficult for a student with anxiety to acquire the correct form of treatment as the extent of their disorder is either not believed by others, or they have a hard time, in general, finding the most effective treatment for themselves. Research supports the idea that, ". . . compared to anxious youth who did not receive treatment, youth who received cognitive behavioral therapy showed improvements in academic motivation (qtd. in Keough et al.), standardizes test scores (qtd. in Keough et al.), GPA (qtd. in Weems et al.), and teacher and parent ratings of general academic functioning" (Nail et al. 329). It is vital for those with medically diagnosed anxiety to undergo treatment as it can not only improve their personal well-being, but also improve their academic success and prevent them from falling behind in school. Receiving treatment can further be translated into having better academic success in college as well; an increase in academic motivation will allow the students to perform well in their classes by not only scoring higher on exams and receiving higher grades, but also increasing their knowledge and understanding of what they learn. Thus, college courses related to these high school topics will become easier for students who struggle with anxiety.

Understanding the challenges of living with medically diagnosed anxiety is important in America's society as 2.2% of adolescents aged 13-18 are diagnosed with GAD, and 9.1% of adolescents are diagnosed with SAD ("Social Anxiety Disorder"). Students are faced with struggles every day as they anticipate the worst of their fears and are forced to protect themselves in a state of caution. Due to this cautious response, a student's academic progress is negatively-effected as their anxiety lessons their ability to work in a school environment.

IV. Discussion

As someone who struggles with anxiety, I believe that it is vital to understand what those with medically diagnosed anxiety go through on a daily basis in school. This report has proved that anxiety is not easy to control as it can be detrimental to a high school student's academic progress. Anxiety could potentially cause a student to drop out of high school, which further affects their future. Without a high school diploma, a student will not be able to attend college and may find it hard to apply for certain jobs in the long-run. Overall, I demonstrate empathy for those with medically diagnosed anxiety because I feel as though I can relate to them and have experienced the same troubles.

What matters most is providing the right help for those with anxiety. One of the most common ways people deal with anxiety is by taking a medication. Although the medication will not cure the disorder, it can lessen the symptoms and make one's life less troublesome. Common medications that can be taken are anti-anxiety medications and antidepressants. Since these medications are prescribed, one must consult a doctor beforehand. Consulting with a doctor may also allow the patient to receive help and guidance with choosing the right medication (APA).

Although medications will not treat anxiety, a common way that will is psychotherapy. One example of psychotherapy is Cognitive Behavioral Therapy (CBT). With this routine, a psychologist helps to identify one's negative thinking and behavior patterns that could be causing harm and worsening their anxiety. The psychologist, in turn, will help their patient develop skills and a different outlook to prevent their anxiety and change the way they respond to certain situations (APA).

Works Cited

Asgari, Masoumeh, et al. "Prevalence of Social Phobia Disorder in High School Students in Abhar City, Iran." *Journal of Fundamentals of Mental Health*, vol. 18, no. 1, Jan. 2016, pp. 42–47. *Academic Search Premier*, search.ebscohost.com/login. aspx?direct=true&db=aph&AN=117066905&site=ehost-live&scope=site.

Fisher, Paige H., et al. "Skills for Social and Academic Success: A School-Based Intervention for Social Anxiety Disorder in Adolescents." *Clinical Child & Family Psychology Review*, vol. 7, no. 4, Dec. 2004, pp. 241–249. *Academic Search Premier*, doi:10.1007/s10567-004-6088-7.

Mehtalia, Khyati, and G. K. Vankar. "Social Anxiety in Adolescents." *Indian Journal of Psychiatry*, vol. 46, no. 3, July 2004, pp. 221–227. *PubMed*, search.ebscohost.com/login.aspx?direct=true&db=cmedm&AN=21224903&site=ehost-live&scope=site.

Pawluk, Elizabeth J., and Naomi Koerner. "The Relationship between Negative Urgency and Generalized Anxiety Disorder Symptoms: The Role of Intolerance of Negative Emotions and Intolerance of Uncertainty." *Anxiety, Stress & Coping*, vol. 29, no. 6, Nov. 2016, pp. 606–615. *Academic Search Premier*, doi:10.1080/10615806.2015.1134786.

Mazzone, Luigi, et al. "The Role of Anxiety Symptoms in School Performance in a Community Sample of Children and Adolescents." *BMC Public Health*, vol. 7, no. 1, 5 Dec. 2007, pp. 1–6. *PubMed*, doi:10.1186/1471-2458-7-347.

Nail, Jennifer, et al. "Academic Impairment and Impact of Treatments Among Youth with Anxiety Disorders." *Child & Youth Care Forum*, vol. 44, no. 3, June 2015, pp. 327–342. *Academic Search Premier*, doi:10.1007/s10566-014-9290-x.

"What Are Anxiety Disorders?" *American Psychiatric Association*, www.psychiatry.org/patients-families/anxiety-disorders/what-are-anxiety-disorders.

"Generalized Anxiety Disorder." *National Institute of Mental Health*, U.S. Department of Health and Human Services, https://www.nimh.nih.gov/health/statistics/generalized-anxiety-disorder.shtml.

"Social Anxiety Disorder." *National Institute of Mental Health*, U.S. Department of Health and Human Services, https://www.nimh.nih.gov/health/statistics/social-anxiety-disorder.shtml.